PRAISE FOR

THE FIVE CHARACTERISTICS
OF A SUCCESSFUL ENTREPRENEUR

"This book is pure gold."

—Randy Garn, New York Times Bestseller

". . . an insightful, captivating read."

—Godard Abel, CEO of SteelBrick and
former CEO of BigMachines.

"Ryan and Travis succinctly summarize data from successful business founders and CEOs in an easy-to-digest way that both seasoned and budding entrepreneurs will find useful."

—Jonathan Johnson, Chairman of Overstock.com

"5 Characteristics is a compelling, in-depth look into the qualities that successful entrepreneurs possess. A must-read!"

—Mark Sunday, SVP & CIO for a major
enterprise software company

"This book not only describes the characteristics of successful entrepreneurs, but it also provides insightful, real-world advice on how to develop them. A compelling read."

—Jeremy Andrus, CEO of Traeger and
former CEO of Skullcandy

THE FIVE CHARACTERISTICS OF A SUCCESSFUL ENTREPRENEUR

THE FIVE
CHARACTERISTICS
OF A SUCCESSFUL
ENTREPRENEUR

RYAN WESTWOOD
TRAVIS JOHNSON

Copyright © 2015
by Ryan Westwood and Travis Johnson

ISBN 978-1-937458-88-1
Library of Congress Control Number: 2015956346
Visit www.sourcedmediabooks.com

DEDICATION

From Ryan Westwood

To Erin Westwood, the yin to my yang, my best friend and wife of ten years, who has believed in me and encouraged me from day one.

To Brad and Virlie Westwood, my parents who raised me and taught me that anything is possible in this world. They taught me to pray, love, laugh, and work hard. Their examples and sacrifice have made me who I am today.

To my encouraging brother, Isaac Westwood, who always has my back.

To my grandpa, Roland Vincent, who taught me how to work hard, have fun, and love the world we live in.

To my grandmas, Sybil Vincent and Yvonne Westwood, who showed me and taught me strength, charity, love, and encouragement.

To my coauthor, Travis Johnson, my first investor and a man I will be forever grateful for, who taught me everything I know about timing and getting things done.

To David Griffin, for encouraging me to quit my job to live the American Dream and become an entrepreneur.

From Travis Johnson

To Kim, my best friend and my wife of twenty-five years. You are my inspiration for being a better person.

To Darby Smith, my business partner and friend for twenty years.

To Ryan Westwood, my business partner, friend, and a real example of being a leader in business and in life.

CONTENTS

INTRODUCTION

For as long as I can remember, I've wanted to work for myself, to be my own boss. While I love learning, growing, and improving, it has long seemed to me that the real action takes place outside the classroom.

When I was a fifth-grader at Sunset Elementary School, I remember feeling frustrated that all of my assignments were given to me by someone else. Although I understood school was mandatory and eventually would transition to a career, I was impatient. I wanted to do something other than just take orders from my teacher.

One day I decided to solve this problem myself. I walked out of school early, hopped on my bike, and rode over to the local Russ Coin to rent a portable kiosk. My plan was to sell my baseball and basketball cards to other kids as they walked home from school.

I had already made a fairly thorough inventory of my collection using the latest Beckett pricing guide, and I added price tags to each card. As a fifth-grader, I was ready—ready to start hustling and bringing home the bacon.

All of my hard work paid off almost instantly. As soon as the final school bell sounded and my schoolmates streamed out of school, I began selling my collectible cards—and turning a healthy profit in the process. Best of all, I seemed to have a lot of happy customers. I could not have imagined a better start for my new assignment working for myself.

Then, around five o'clock, with my sidewalk business still booming, I saw a familiar face walking toward me.

"Where have you been today?" my father demanded to know, a mix of anger and relief on his face. "I heard you weren't at school."

"I've been selling my cards, Dad," I replied, gesturing to my sidewalk stand. "I've been working."

He chuckled. "You can't just leave school, Ryan."

"But school's so boring, Dad."

"That may be. But you need to get an education, Son."

I knew a losing argument when I saw one. Dejected, I packed up my kiosk and went home with my father. I didn't know if or when I'd have another chance to launch an endeavor like this, but I knew that someday, somehow, I wanted to be the one calling the shots. I wanted to be an entrepreneur.

The Importance of Doing

As students in our modern education system, we spend a lot of time waiting for our teachers to tell us what to do. Our teachers set a highly regimented daily schedule, and we live by it. Our teachers set the rules, and we (more or less) live by them. Our teachers determine the curriculum, and we live by it.

This is all done with good reason, of course. The American education system is set up to instill knowledge and wisdom and, perhaps just as importantly, to help us learn how to accept and fulfill assignments that others give us. But as a student going through the system, I couldn't help but notice that it does little to foster the entrepreneurial spirit of America—you know, the spirit that throughout history has moved our society forward in leaps and bounds.

Looking back, what I realized is that school doesn't teach you *how* to do. "I have been impressed with the urgency of doing," Renaissance artist Leonardo da Vinci once said. "Knowing is not enough; we must apply. Being willing is not enough; we must do."

As a newly minted college grad, I realized how little value I could bring to the workplace with just my education. Yes, I was presumably better equipped to do more than sell some baseball cards and had gained incredible academic knowledge and perspective. But I didn't feel my education had "taught" me how to do business and certainly not how to do the work of an entrepreneur.

So I decided I would learn how to work for myself using the same strategy I'd used in elementary school: jump right in and just start doing. And that's exactly what I did.

At the same time that I began moving up the ranks of corporate America, I launched a company that sells vending art supplies. I got the idea simply by looking at what college art students needed. They would frequently run out of art supplies, but—since they were poor college students—few of them wanted to buy their supplies from the school at premium prices. So I decided to start selling art supplies to these students at lower prices.

The business took off immediately, and within just six months, I sold the company for three times the revenue I was bringing in. This eye-opening experience reaffirmed for me how incredibly rewarding it is to be an entrepreneur, to be truly "doing." And, best of all, it was way better than working for "the man." I saved my money and left my corporate job as soon as I could to focus all of my time on starting more businesses.

As I reflect back on my early days in the art supply business, what's most interesting to me is that I'm sure I'm not the only one who has thought it might be smart to sell supplies to art students. It's probably a safe bet that I wasn't even the tenth or twentieth person to think of it, maybe not even the fiftieth. The only difference in this case between the fiftieth person and the first forty-nine is that the fiftieth didn't let his idea stay an idea. He actually started doing something about it.

Perhaps no person in American history better personifies the "get 'er done" entrepreneurial spirit than Thomas Edison. Despite having just three months of formal schooling, Edison became a highly productive inventor with more than 1,000 patents to his name. Many of these inventions—like the light bulb, phonograph, motion picture camera, and stock ticker—have had a profound impact on the modern world. And it was all because he was a doer.

Indeed, the "Wizard of Menlo Park" was more than just your garden-variety mad scientist tinkering in an attic lab with all of his spare time. Edison was a highly motivated and successful entrepreneur who understood how to parlay his remarkable inventions into outsized business success stories. Edison founded fourteen companies, including one (General Electric) whose appliances you might have in your kitchen.

Entire books can (and have) been written about how he managed to be so successful. To me, one of the most basic and often overlooked secrets to his success is the simple fact that he was a doer. The reason so many people miss out on great business opportunities, he once noted, is that those opportunities are "dressed in overalls and [look] like work."

And he's right. Most of us struggle to see the entrepreneurial potential in the ideas right in front of us. "Being busy does not always mean real work," Edison said. "The object of all work is production or accomplishment."

Even so, not every entrepreneur who runs with her ideas ultimately finds success. Why is it, then, that some entrepreneurs and business leaders are able to achieve the elusive degree of "production or accomplishment" that Edison spoke of, while others flounder? What do the world's most successful business leaders do that others don't?

At its most basic level, this gets to the heart of why my long-time business partner Travis and I wrote this book. We know how frustrating it can be when we, as business leaders, find ourselves working very hard on something, only to realize later that our efforts and energies might have been better spent elsewhere. Sometimes there just doesn't seem to be a rhyme or a reason for business successes and failures. But there must be, right?

Thinking in Numbers

Throughout our professional lives—no matter how many times we found success in our own careers—Travis and I have been motivated by the question of why some entrepreneurs find runaway success while others struggle. Surely the most successful among us must be doing things that our less successful counterparts are not doing—or vice versa.

Every time we would meet a successful colleague, we would reflect back on that encounter together and try to explain to ourselves what has made her successful. Similarly, every time we would pick up a book written by a successful entrepreneur, we would look for the magic ingredient, the underlying keys to this author's success. Try as we might, we struggled to put our finger on how to synthesize what we'd learned into something meaningful and definitive and concrete—something that could personally satisfy our insatiable curiosity.

Being business-minded professionals, you see, Travis and I think in numbers. Anecdotal information has always frustrated us because it's not quantifiable; indeed, we've never been able to get around the fact that quantifying personal observations and experiences—even in lengthy books—necessarily skews reality and makes any conclusions drawn prone to bias and subjectivity. In other words, there's never a way to trust observations and analysis that are drawn from someone's personal anecdotes.

This shortcoming got us thinking about how to scientifically quantify the must-know characteristics of a successful entrepreneur. We studied a number of different approaches that business researchers and psychologists have taken to answer this question. What we found is that they tend to use a narrower list of personality characteristics as their starting point. Then they conduct an analysis seeking to understand the relative importance and interplay of those characteristics.

We realized we wanted to take a different tactic. Our idea was to let the entrepreneurs themselves tell us what kinds of characteristics are important for succeeding as an entrepreneur. After scouring books and the Internet, it became clear that no one had designed a study similar to what we'd envisioned. So I told Travis we should do just what we'd always done: Step away from the proverbial classroom and just start doing. As we started solidifying our ideas, we realized we could create a product that others have no doubt thought about but have never pursued— the very essence of what sets entrepreneurs apart from the rest, right?

Our brainstorming ultimately coalesced around designing a survey that would incorporate solid statistical principles and hold up to the rigor around which leading U.S. polling firms get a pulse on the nation's mood and views.

After months of careful consideration, research, and consultation, we emailed our survey to 100,000 U.S.

entrepreneurs. We asked them a series of questions designed to gauge their views about just one subject: What do the most successful U.S. entrepreneurs believe are the five characteristics essential for success?

Designing Our Survey

One of the most fundamental parameters of designing our survey was deciding who to send it to. Indeed, Travis and I fully recognized there are different ways to define business success that vary widely from person to person. We decided to focus on the folks who had achieved an indisputably high level of accomplishment: the business CEOs and founders who have presided over an entity that has earned at least $1 million in annual revenue.

Why did we restrict our survey only to business CEOs and founders? First, we're both CEOs and founders ourselves, so we were most interested in learning how our peers felt. Second, only CEOs and founders can fully appreciate the nuances and struggles of running a business—particularly a small startup business.

We decided on the $1 million threshold as our cutoff to make sure we were receiving responses from those who have achieved an objective, quantifiable level of success. Although we could have set the bar much higher, we did not want to exclude those who have found their success under the radar, so to speak—the talented, unsung heroes whose names haven't (yet!) appeared on any Fortune 500 lists.

We also wanted to get responses from leaders who have been in the game for a long time. Of course we were interested in hearing from younger entrepreneurs who have been at it for a few years, as well as those who have been at it just a few months. But we believe there is a great deal of wisdom that only time and experience can teach. "A man who carries a cat by the tail learns something he can learn in no other way," Mark Twain once observed in his always witty, humorous style.

Because we wanted to think through every possible nuance, we also decided to compare the responses of the elder statesmen of the business world to those of their younger counterparts. Do they think fundamentally differently? A statistical comparison would help us to find out.

In the end, we looked at our survey data in a number of ways. We ran correlations among the top five characteristics of successful entrepreneurs, looked at relationships and variances of the five characteristics in relation to other variables, and assessed the certainty with which we could state our results. Each statistical analysis we performed put us one step closer to satiating our numbers-oriented, entrepreneurial brains.

Seeking Wisdom from Predecessors

Imagine you have set a goal to climb Mount Everest, the highest mountain peak in the world. You spend a year training, getting in shape, and making travel accommodations. You make the trip to Tibet and reach the base of the mountain, only to find that the altitude acclimation camps set up all along the grueling trek are suddenly gone. There are also no Sherpa guides to help you. The ropes and markers that let you know you are headed in the right direction are nowhere to be found. Who would continue their trek under those conditions? Only the most foolish, right?

The same is true in the entrepreneurial business world. Those who forego the wisdom of their predecessors are destined to fall off a craggy, icy cliff. That's why we must take advantage of the wisdom of entrepreneurial leaders; we need to soak it up and use it strategically to mimic their successes.

Receiving more than 2,600 responses to our survey was a humbling, eye-opening experience for us. Although some of the things we learned confirmed things that our own business experiences have taught us over the years, we were awed by all of the interesting new perspectives gleaned from the written comments our survey respondents shared with us—perspectives that no amount of personal anecdotal experience could ever teach a person.

Of course, what Travis and I learned from others will do the most good if you're willing to truly absorb it and make corresponding changes in your own life. C.S. Lewis expressed this internal struggle perfectly when he said, "It may be hard for an egg to turn into a bird: It would be a jolly sight harder for it to learn to fly while remaining an egg. We are like eggs at present. And you cannot go on indefinitely being just an ordinary, decent egg. We must be hatched or go bad."

In that spirit, this analysis of the five essential characteristics of entrepreneurial success is really about helping entrepreneurs and business leaders of every stripe transform our ordinary egg selves into hatched birds that can soar to great heights.

Our hope is that this labor of love will help you to become a better leader, entrepreneur, and business person. We hope you'll react to the survey findings like we did— with equal parts surprise, understanding, and excitement.

Just as importantly, we hope this book will reinforce for you why there has never been a better time to be an entrepreneur. Like every great entrepreneurial leader who has come before us, we all just need a steady guiding hand along the way.

KEYS TO SUCCESS

"Sometimes life is about risking it all for a dream no one can see but you."

– Anonymous

Anyone looking for advice on how to succeed as an entrepreneur is certain to find it—too much of it.

"Spend money where it counts. Be ultra-frugal where you can."

"Take everything as an opportunity to learn and grow."

"Make a difference . . . Money will follow."

"Nothing in this world can take the place of persistence."

It goes without saying that no matter how well-intentioned some folks are, dishing out an overabundance of business advice is overwhelming. And, indeed, it seems that every entrepreneur you talk to will define success a little differently.

THE 5 CHARACTERISTICS OF A SUCCESSFUL ENTREPRENEUR

(In fact, each of the nuggets of advice above are actual words of wisdom from business CEOs and founders who were kind enough to share their insights with us in our survey.)

How, then, are entrepreneurs supposed to translate this cacophony into an insightful takeaway message they can apply to their business pursuits? And for that matter, what is the most universal advice that seasoned pros should be offering to the next generation of entrepreneurs? The next generation will need this wisdom, delivered with a level of consistency and reliability they can use.

Like our peers before us, Travis and I have dished out plenty of well-intentioned words of wisdom over the years—despite not knowing whether what we were saying was going to be truly useful to someone else. The root of the problem, we realized, was that this advice has always been anecdotal.

Researchers and psychologists have spent decades working to dissect, analyze, and zero in on the personality characteristics that are intrinsic to entrepreneurs and entrepreneurial success. They have amassed a sizeable body of scholarly work in their efforts to understand which characteristics seem to be unique to entrepreneurs, which characteristics seem to be associated with successful vs. unsuccessful entrepreneurs, and which characteristics are correlated with specific entrepreneurial skill sets.

Some have posited, for example, that the basic elements of entrepreneurship are perception, courage, and action.[1]

---

1 - Hébert, Robert F., and Albert N. Link. "In search of the meaning of entrepreneurship." *Small Business Economics* 1.1 (1989): 39-49.

14

Others have suggested that the key characteristics distinguishing true entrepreneurs from managers with similar responsibilities are risk-taking propensity, locus of control, energy level, and need for achievement.[2]

Still other studies have approached the question by defining a set of personality characteristics to examine and then conducting a rigorous analysis seeking to draw meaningful insights about the particular set of characteristics. A seminal 2004 study of U.S. entrepreneurs, for example, analyzed their impressions of the relative importance of the Big Five personality traits—openness, conscientiousness, extraversion, agreeableness, and neuroticism—which psychologists believe are at the core of every individual's personality.[3] In a follow-up 2011 study, researchers investigated the role these same Big Five traits play in entrepreneurial failure.[4]

A 2004 British study of entrepreneurs, meanwhile, looked at the relative importance of six characteristics associated with entrepreneurship: focus, advantage, creativity, ego, team, and social.[5] And a 1999 Dutch study that sought to build a personality test capable of assessing an entrepreneur's likelihood for success started by weighing three main characteristics (achievement, internal locus of control, and risk-taking propensity) and five secondary

2 - Naffziger, Douglas. "Entrepreneurship: A person based theory approach." *Advances in Entrepreneurship, Firm Emergence, and Growth* 2 (1995): 21-50.

3 - Ciavarella, Mark A., et al. "The Big Five and venture survival: Is there a linkage?" *Journal of Business Venturing* 19.4 (2004): 465-483.

4 - Cantner, Uwe, Rainer K. Silbereisen, and Sebastian Wilfling. "Which Big-Five personality traits drive entrepreneurial failure in highly innovative industries?" Paper presented at the DIME Final Conference. Vol. 6. 2011.

5 - Thompson, John L. "The facets of the entrepreneur: Identifying entrepreneurial potential." *Management Decision* 42.2 (2004): 243-258.

characteristics (autonomy, power, tolerance of ambiguity, affiliation, and endurance).[6]

What becomes clear from looking at this body of work is that researchers have worked in earnest over the years to identify the personality characteristics associated with entrepreneurial success. What also becomes clear is that there is little consensus about which characteristics are associated with entrepreneurial success, or about what wisdom business schools and mentors and colleagues should be imparting to the next generation of entrepreneurs.

That's how Travis and I decided to tackle this issue from a different perspective. We would ask the entrepreneurs themselves. Working with an expert team of researchers and academic colleagues, we designed a web survey inviting 100,000 business CEOs and company founders to identify the top five personality characteristics of successful entrepreneurs. We scoured the literature on this subject to develop a large, inclusive list of personality characteristics from which they could choose—or they were welcome to write in their own.

Unveiling the Results

When Travis and I first conceptualized our survey of CEOs a few years ago, we knew we didn't want to rely on just the perspectives of our friends and colleagues, or even just our local Utah business community. We wanted to blanket the entire country with our survey.

---

6 - Driessen, Martyn P., and Peter S. Zwart. "The role of the entrepreneur in small business success: The Entrepreneurship Scan." 44th ICSB World Conference Proceedings Innovation and Economic Development: the Role of Entreprenuership and SMEs, Nápoles. (1999).

Hence, we purchased a list of contact information for 100,000 U.S. business CEOs and company founders inviting them to anonymously select the top five most important characteristics for entrepreneurial success. Our survey was returned by 2,691 respondents, 98% of which were valid.

The results blew away our wildest expectations. Not only did our team of analysts assure us that we had achieved statistically significant results, but there was also one characteristic selected by a majority of respondents.

What was this characteristic that was elevated on such a high pedestal?

Vision, selected by 61% of survey respondents. Vision is the gift of being able to see into one's future, of being able to develop a clear path forward in the quest to accomplish lofty goals and ambitions. It's with vision that we're inspired to push through our insecurities, fears, and uncertainties to ultimately succeed.

"If it's vision you lack, imagine a road trip without a map," one of our survey respondents commented. "Yes, it's exciting at the start, but you could easily run out of gas without a map of where you're heading."

The other top five most commonly selected characteristics of successful entrepreneurs were, in order, work ethic (45%), resilience (42%), positivity (35%), and passion (34%).

Each of these five characteristics was selected by at least 30% of respondents.

That is in contrast to the five least selected characteristics—influence, frugality, attention to detail, caring, and money management—that were all selected by 10% or less of respondents. The spread was remarkable to us. Our survey respondents were clearly trying to tell us some characteristics are far more important than others.

While it's fascinating to ponder why entrepreneurs dismissed the least selected characteristics, our main focus was on understanding which characteristics were most likely to be selected. In fact, we've devoted the next five chapters of this book to exploring these top five characteristics.

After we take you through each of the five characteristics, we'll examine how you can live the five characteristics in your daily lives and work. Then we'll offer our concluding thoughts about what this process has taught us and what we hope you'll take away from this book.

As you continue your journey to entrepreneurial success, please keep in mind that the top five characteristics of entrepreneurial success aren't intended as a single, definitive formula for success. Entrepreneurs can (and do) come from any place and any field, and the ingenious strategies and solutions they develop can change the world in a variety of ways.

In this book, we will explore some of the key statistical commonalities among successful entrepreneurs—and ultimately gain meaningful insights into the incredibly rich fabric that makes up the most successful among us.

VISION: THE NUMBER ONE KEY TO SUCCESS

"The greatest danger for most of us is not that our aim is too high and we miss it, but that it is too low and we reach it."

– Attributed to Michelangelo

Close your eyes and think about something you really want. It might be a goal you want to achieve today, tomorrow, or ten years from now. It could be something material, such as a new car, a date with your spouse this weekend, or a vacation to the Bahamas. Or it could be something more intangible, such as a better relationship or more quality time spent with family.

Keep your eyes closed and take a few moments to imagine the moment it becomes real. Now, open your eyes and write down your goal on a piece of paper, along with answers to the following questions:

1. *How will you feel when it is fully within your grasp?*
2. *Why is it so important to you?*
3. *If it's something that will take a long time to achieve, what are some smaller accomplishments along the way that will tell you that you're on your way to achieving this goal?*
4. *What steps are you going to take to get there?*
5. *How will you know for certain you have accomplished the goal?*

What you'll see on this piece of paper is a vision. Vision plays a transformative role in ensuring we do the things we set out to achieve, creating a roadmap to success that influences our thoughts, feelings, attitudes, and behavior.

Vision is also the single most important characteristic of entrepreneurial success, picked by 61% of business CEOs and founders who responded to our survey.

As you outlined your vision on paper, think about the way it made your mind churn. You undoubtedly realized you need to make changes in your life if you truly want to see your vision realized. Although creating this vision may have made you feel fear and uncertainty, the desire to achieve your goal probably far outweighed your self-doubting and made you feel inspired to push through whatever is necessary to achieve it. This is the interminable power of vision.

In this chapter, we'll start by sharing what we learned about vision from our survey of 2,631 business CEOs and founders. This will set us up for a deeper discussion about the common pitfalls associated with vision—that is, failing to create an all-encompassing vision or making excuses to delay developing one. Then we'll move into the how-to phase of developing a vision as we share with you what we believe to be the most powerful, effective strategy for building a vision and setting up your company to achieve this vision.

What Our Survey Reveals about Vision

In our survey of business CEOs and founders, 61% of the 2,631 respondents chose vision as essential to entrepreneurial success. Indeed, it was the only characteristic that was identified by a majority of the respondents.

This finding marked a turning point in our research. We'd always believed that having a vision was important, but realizing that so many of our peers felt so strongly about vision gave us newfound perspective. We had stumbled across something remarkable: the most important key to entrepreneurial success is vision.

As we continued to examine what the data revealed, we became even more intrigued by the ways that vision stood apart from the other characteristics—in particular, the top five most frequently selected characteristics of vision, work ethic, resilience, positivity, and passion. A statistical correlation analysis showed that vision stood apart from these four other characteristics in that it was not closely correlated with any other particular characteristics from the list.

By this we mean that when a respondent picked "vision," a correlation analysis was unable to establish which other characteristics the respondent was likely to choose. By contrast, there were particularly strong correlations among respondents who picked resilience; they were likely to also pick drive and focus. And respondents who chose passion were likely to also choose positive attitude.

The takeaway message here is that vision seems to be a more universal, essential characteristic than any other. No matter what else respondents said was important, vision was most likely to rise to the top.

"If you believe strongly enough in your idea and vision, do everything you can to make it happen," one of our survey respondents shared with us.

Once we understood that vision was so widely viewed as crucial, we wanted to drill down even deeper into our data. We asked, "Is vision only important to entrepreneurs who are just getting their start, or does it transcend company age, as well?"

Surprisingly, it turned out to be the latter. Vision was picked by entrepreneurs who have been in business for sixteen or more years almost as frequently as it was selected by entrepreneurs who have been in business just two to five years. The bracket next most likely to select vision was the grouping of entrepreneurs who have been in business eleven to fifteen years.

Survey respondents with a year or less of experience were least likely to select vision. It's hard to say why, but thinking back to our early entrepreneurial days, we can remember how overwhelming everything felt. Indeed, if we had been asked to fill out our own survey as nascent entrepreneurs, we would have felt similarly unsure what to pick! (A subanalysis of data from the CEOs and founders with less than a year under their belt seemed to confirm our intuition. They picked from among all of the characteristics with close to equal frequency.)

"It may take years of that fluctuation before you achieve success," one survey respondent commented. "There may come a time, years after you found your company, that you are in a low, but it is the entrepreneur who perseveres and is able to continue to push forward, who ultimately succeeds."

Despite the clarity and forcefulness of this message, Travis and I are constantly surprised at the number of floundering entrepreneurs we encounter who are lacking in vision. They don't seem to have received the most important memo of all.

When You Have No Vision

Everyone knows the story of *Alice in Wonderland*, the classic Lewis Carroll tale about a curious girl who falls down a rabbit hole and, unable to find her way, stumbles upon the Cheshire Cat.

"Would you tell me, please, which way I ought to go from here?" Alice asks.

"That depends a good deal on where you want to get to," the Cat replies.

"I don't much care where—"

"Then it doesn't matter which way you go."[1]

---

1 - Carroll, Lewis. *Alice in Wonderland* (London: 1865).

As children, we understood Alice's problem to be quite obvious. She had no vision of where she wanted to go, so of course no one could help her get there.

As adults, we have the same problem; it's just that we don't always have the ability to see it. In business especially, we hear all too often an entrepreneur who says that he wants to achieve success by building a "good company" and having "satisfied clients." When these vague statements aren't followed up by something specific and concrete, they are signs that an entrepreneur lacks a true vision. If we cannot articulate a clear picture of what our success looks like, then how are we supposed to get to where we want to go?

Early in my career, a close friend of mine worked for a CEO who didn't seem to have any clear sense of direction about where he wanted the company to go or what he wanted to accomplish. Beyond offering the services that the company did, my friend had no idea why it existed. She didn't know if the company had plans to expand to new locations or to hire more employees. She couldn't articulate if the company was aiming to retain 10 new clients this year or 10,000 new clients.

I experienced this same level of frustration in one of my own past jobs. In fact, I could not even use my CEO's list of current projects to gain insights into what our company's vision was—because he couldn't articulate to me where he was going with what he was working on. And I was in upper management!

To illustrate how powerless it feels to not know your employer's vision, imagine being stuck on a lifeboat somewhere in a vast, empty ocean. In any direction you look, there is water as far as the eye can see. Even if you have oars in your lifeboat, what are you going to use them for? Without landmarks of any kind, it is impossible to know which direction to paddle. As nighttime falls, you turn to the stars to help guide you, but the stars can only give you an idea of what direction you might be headed. You need someone to rescue you, and you begin calling out for help.

The lack of vision works the same way. Without one, you end up with a recipe for stagnation, frustration, and failure. As the leader of a business becomes bogged down, he brings down all of his employees with him.

When You Put Off Your Vision

As much as we may value vision, we often make excuses for why we don't have one yet. You have probably heard some version of these excuses before:

"Once I advance a little farther in my career and gain a little more leadership experience, I'll map out a strategic vision."

"As soon as things start to calm down a bit, I'll hold some strategic planning workshops to plot our path forward."

Developing a clear and compelling vision can, for many entrepreneurial leaders, seem like an intimidating and challenging process. There are so many moving parts to starting a new business and so many things in flux that you don't have control over. Hence, it doesn't seem realistic to have a vision when you don't know if you're going to get the $1 million venture capital money you've lobbied for or if you're going to hire the key sales executive candidate you've been courting.

Compounding these fears is that in any organization—even established ones—vision needs to be shared by all of its participants to be truly effective. The larger your company is, the more chaotic things seem and the less control you have over getting your entire team on the same page.[2] You simply put off the inevitable, hoping for a more optimal, less stressful time.

The problem, of course, is that without vision, no business or organization will accomplish anything meaningful. Indeed, Travis and I believe this obstacle plays a huge role in why so many businesses manage to survive and sustain themselves for long periods of time but fail to experience the kind of steady, impressive growth and achievement their owners hope for. As Walmart founder Sam Walton once put it, "Capital isn't scarce; vision is." Walton understood that when you have a strong vision, capital and talent and success will follow.

In the exercise you performed at the beginning of this chapter, you created a vivid mental and emotional experience that gave you a clear sense of what it would take to reach your goals. It became clear to you (hopefully!) that thinking realistically, optimistically, and with great depth about your vision was so much more valuable for you than talking in vague terms about "someday" accomplishing your goal. There was never a question about whether you could make excuses to avoid or postpone achieving your goal. Despite what seems so obvious to us now, many en-

---

2 - Spiro, Josh. "How to get employees excited about your business vision," *Inc,* August 30, 2010. http://www. inc.com/guides/2010/08/how-to-get-employees-excited-about-your-business-vision. html.

trepreneurs don't maintain this focus. They tend to picture excuses instead of opportunities.

As humans, we have long recognized the value of vision, even when the people we turn to for leadership don't have one to share with us. "Where there is no vision, the people perish," the Book of Proverbs in the Bible tells us. In the modern workplace, of course, employees cannot afford to physically just give up—their livelihoods and homes and families are at stake.

At the same time, something curious tends to happen when employees receive no vision from the top. They instinctively figure out what their job should be, and they develop an impromptu, haphazard vision to guide what they think they should be doing. On the one hand, this proactive, healthy thinking is a quality any business should be grateful to have among its ranks. On the other hand, with no unifying force at the top bringing these competing visions together, the company ends up with a very arbitrary, non-cohesive vision of what success looks like.

It goes without saying, then, that the best vision comes from the top. Even if your vision is still a work in progress, or comes with a disclaimer and caveats, a clear strategic institutional vision is better than no vision.

For Travis and me, the most personally rewarding part of having a vision is that when our vision guides us to success, it will give us confidence in our ability to repeat the process. After all, when you're able to accomplish something that has a great deal of personal meaning to you, it's bound to give you wings, propelling you to ever-greater heights.

The V2MOM Formula for Success

Early in my career, when I joined the executive team of a fledgling startup, I thought a lot about establishing a vision that could help us become a better, more focused organization. Seeking to gain insights from those who have come before me, I did a great deal of reading and research.

For me, the ideas of one entrepreneur—Marc Benioff, founder, chairman, and CEO of Salesforce, a global cloud computing giant based in San Francisco—stood out above the rest. His transformative role in guiding Salesforce from a fledgling startup into one of the most respected and widely used brands in the enterprise work management industry is nothing short of miraculous. With Benioff at the helm, Salesforce has been recognized and written about countless times by *The Wall Street Journal*, *Forbes*, *Wired*, *BusinessWeek*, and others.

Before Benioff found his runaway success, though, he was just another talented, idealistic entrepreneur like the rest of us. During his tenure as a vice president for the information technology giant Oracle, Benioff says he struggled with the fact that the company did not have a written business plan.

Benioff's lightbulb moment came, he says, when he realized that having no vision for where you want to go is going to prevent you from ending up anywhere you want to be. It's the same lesson Alice learned from the Cheshire Cat!

Benioff's quest to provide clarity and purpose to the work he was doing led to the development of a leadership framework that he calls the V2MOM. This acronym, which stands for Vision, Values, Methods, Obstacles, Measures, provides a way for business leaders to organize their visions into a simple, meaningful, and measurable road-map to success.[3]

Travis and I have used the V2MOM with great success, and we believe it's so universally applicable that any business can benefit from it. In the next sections, we will walk you through each of the five elements of the V2MOM framework and share with you from our perspective how to apply the V2MOM framework to your business. I also will share with you specific examples of how I used V2MOM when I founded PcCareSupport, a Utah tech company that provides computer software, service, and tech support to businesses and individuals.

Vision

Vision, the first and most important section of the V2MOM formula, is an opportunity for you to define what you do in the clearest terms possible. Not only does vision represent what you aspire to, but it also represents a standard against which to measure everything your company does.

When I started PcCareSupport and wrote my V2MOM, my vision statement reflected my goal to grow it into a world-class tech support company that could be sold within five years. The specificity and non-ambiguity of this vision made many of the decisions about the future

---

3 - Benioff, Marc. "How to create alignment within your company in order to succeed" Salesforce Blog, April 9, 2013. https://www.Salesforce.com/blog/2013/04/how-to-create-alignment-within-your-company.html.

of my company much easier to make than they otherwise would have been. Anytime we were considering taking on a new project or direction, we would always weigh this proposal against our vision statement. Would it move us closer to our vision or not? When viewed through this lens, the answer most of the time became a no-brainer.

As you look to write your own organization's vision statement, the key question to answer is simple: What do you want?

In my case, what I wanted for PcCareSupport was simply stated and easily measurable. Our financial statements would make it clear when we had grown into a company worth a few million in EBITDA, as well as if we were on track for a sale within the four-year mark.

You may find that a less specific vision statement than mine is better suited for your company's needs. When Benioff drafted Salesforce's first V2MOM, he wrote that the company's vision was to "rapidly create a world-class internet company/site for sales force automation."

If your vision statement ends up being less specific, like the Salesforce vision statement, our recommendation is to not make it so broad that there is confusion about what your company wants to accomplish. In the Salesforce statement, for example, it is clear that the company wants to focus on one thing: being a world-class provider of online sales force automation.

I can imagine that Salesforce would have ended up in a very different place if Benioff had stated that his vision was to create a world-class company that provides important tools for businesses. His company would have taken on a very different set of projects and priorities that would have shaped it into a very different company—and perhaps not the hugely successful, widely admired company it is today.

Values

The second section of the V2MOM framework asks you to set forth the principles and beliefs necessary for your company to live out its vision. As you ponder defining your company's values, ask yourself: What is the most important thing about your vision? Perhaps it's the opportunity to create a top-notch organization, or the chance to produce a product or service that will make something easier for businesses or consumers, or the ability to foster a certain kind of culture within your company. Values stem directly from the company's vision and offer your company a foundation to shape this vision.

At the same time, keep in mind that values are not synonymous with goals, nor are they the vision itself. This can be a tricky concept. When I founded PcCareSupport, we stated our values this way:

1. Have accountability.

2. Be creative (ideas win—not titles!).

3. Always ask: What channels can we use to drive PcCareSupport to the market?

4. Provide service with a smile.

5. Take time to celebrate.

6. Sell with integrity.

7. Foster a positive culture.

Here's another way of thinking about what values are. Values determine what standards we use on a day-to-day basis to determine whether we are becoming the kind of company we want to become. While vision points us in the right direction and tells us where we want to go, values tell us what kind of people and what kind of organization we will be.

Write values that your management team buys into and ideally helps you craft. If your management team doesn't act in a way that is reflective of the company's values, then you run the risk of your employees losing faith in the validity of the entire V2MOM process.

Methods

The third section of the V2MOM informs what tactics or strategies you will use to fulfill your vision. Whereas your vision tells you where you want to go, and your values explain what kind of an organization you will be on your way there, your methods describe how you will get there.

As you ponder writing your methods, ask yourself: What are the actions or steps that everyone on your team will take to ensure that you reach your vision? Although this can seem like an overwhelming question—it is impossible, after all, to describe every single thing that will be done along the way—it can often help business leaders divide the methods section into sub-sections.

When I founded PcCareSupport, I divided our methods section into three sub-sections: business-to-business, inside sales, and operations. Underneath each, I listed key tactics and strategies that we would use to fulfill our vision. I organized our V2MOM methods as follows:

Business-to-Business

1. Have four outside sales territories (unless we focus on lead generation and new partners).

2. Increase Google AdWords leads for outside sales.

3. Generate ninety leads per month in each territory.

4. Focus on lead flow.

5. Cross-train business side of ISPs.

6. Launch a newsletter that strengthens customer relationships and drives a lead source.

Inside Sales

1. Have four ISP partners.

2. Find a way to generate revenue with ISP install teams.

Operations

1. Salesforce function, with each employee understanding it.

2. Hire lead generation manager.

3. Technology consultants (hire, train, commissions in Salesforce).

For many businesses, writing the methods section in a very specific manner—as you can see we did at PcCare-Support—makes it easier to think about which methods will help you get closer to your vision and which will not. Part of my motivation for making PcCareSupport's methods statement as thorough and as clear as possible was to ensure that each of the three departments—business-to-business, inside sales, and operations—would not have any concerns about which of the methods apply to their primary spheres of responsibility. In addition, writing our methods section this way enabled people in each department to see what those in other departments were working on.

A carefully written methods section also can break down barriers among divisions of the company. Recall my story about working at a company where, although I was in management, I wasn't able to gain insight into what the CEO was working on. The surprisingly powerful detachment I felt—of being left out of the loop, so to speak—powered my desire to write a methods section for PcCareSupport that would ensure nobody in our company ever had a reason to feel detached. Clearly delineating which department would focus on each of our methods was one of the ways we were able to prevent this noxious culture from gaining a foothold in our company.

As important as it was for our company to make this section as clear and detailed as we could, other leaders in other companies, who face their own unique situations and challenges, may prefer a less specific approach. At Benioff's company, for example, the Salesforce V2MOM did not specify which methods were the primary responsibility of which department:

1. Hire the team.

2. Finalize product specification and technical architecture.

3. Develop the product specification to beta and production stages.

4. Build partnerships with big e-commerce, content, and hosting companies.

5. Build a launch plan.

6. Develop exit strategy (IPO/acquisition).

Whether you choose to divide your methods among departments or to simply create one master methods list, the most important things to do are to make sure your methods align with your vision and to list them all in order of priority. You want to make sure these methods are prioritized in a way that makes it clear which ones will have the greatest impact on your ability to reach your vision.

As Travis and I look back on the methods section that I initially wrote for PcCareSupport, we can't help but chuckle at some of the naïve statements I incorporated into this section. What I've learned is that it's OK to not have all the answers. The important thing is to codify your methods in a written V2MOM as best you can.

Obstacles

The fourth V2MOM section asks you to define the difficulties, problems and other issues you anticipate becoming roadblocks to accomplishing your vision. The obstacles section is built on the important premise that even the most difficult obstacles we face in our professional, personal, religious, and family lives can often be overcome by anticipating them beforehand and taking steps to prepare properly for them.

Mountain climbers who scale a great peak typically research the setting long before they set foot on the mountain. They need to be aware of as many obstacles as they conceivably can, allowing them to bring proper equipment or do the appropriate training they'll need to make a safe, successful climb.

Likewise, individuals and organizations must spend time surveying the situation and making an honest assessment of what problems or difficulties may arise. This does not mean, however, that leaders should get bogged down pointing out every single potential pitfall along the way. Rather, the goal of writing the obstacles section is to force you to think about anticipated problems and viable solutions to overcome them–long before you find yourself mired in the problem.

At PcCareSupport, my obstacles section consisted of a short list outlining key areas in which we anticipated facing challenges:

Operations

1. HTML (we need a web developer).

2. Finance (we absolutely must be dedicated to it).

3. Lead generation.

As with our methods section, the obstacles section allowed us to begin immediately changing how we do many things—changes that might otherwise have only been made once the obstacle had ballooned into a crisis. For example, the simple act of committing to paper that lead generation would potentially be a big obstacle allowed everyone at the company to prioritize it. We were minimizing our risks of an embarrassing, financially distressing situation by planning ahead; we refused to let this issue have a profoundly negative impact on our ability to reach our vision.

And as with your V2MOM values, it is important that you prioritize your obstacles so that it will be clear which ones pose the greatest threat to your vision. Of course, your priorities may fluctuate from month to month, perhaps even from day to day. But it's critical to be aware of which obstacles in the bigger picture are most deserving of the time and energy you spend overcoming them.

Measures

The fifth V2MOM section calls on you to articulate how you will know if you're on the way to achieving your vision. The goal of setting measures is to establish incremental benchmarks and milestones along the way that can tell you when you're on course—and when you slip off course.

I've seen far too many entrepreneurs set out to accomplish their vision without knowing if they are headed in the right direction. The irony is that it would be almost unthinkable to act this way if we were taking a road trip or going on a hike through the forest. We would instinctively and periodically make sure that we were traveling on the right road going the right direction. We'd make use of a map, a GPS device, a smartphone app, whatever we could get our hands on.

That's why it's so peculiar to me to come across an entrepreneur with a grand vision who doesn't think about how he will measure his progress along the way. I wouldn't be surprised if on his road trip to Boston, he would end up over 200 miles away in New York City!

When I wrote the V2MOM Measure section at Pc-CareSupport, I wanted to choose major moments in our growth that we could all agree were indicators we were (or weren't) staying on the path to success. I decided that PcCareSupport would know we had achieved our vision when:

1. We had $94,000 per month in revenues.

2. Salesforce was no longer an inhibitor to our growth.

3. We had developed a culture of accountability.

Benioff kept the V2MOM measures section for Salesforce a little less numbers-oriented. Salesforce's measures consisted of:

1. Prototype is state-of-the-art.

2. High-quality functional system.

3. Partnerships are online and integrated.

4. Salesforce.com is regarded as leader and visionary.

5. We are all rich.

Travis and I cannot emphasize enough the importance of making the path to your vision measurable. Your measures will empower your vision to become more than a pipe dream, providing you with accountability, course corrections, and encouragement. When we set measures, we are forced to reconcile our daily efforts with an unambiguous, unchanging standard dependent on results, not excuses.

Too many entrepreneurs go to great lengths to "explain away" their failures; they justify these failures as part of the progress toward achieving their vision. That's what is so valuable about an objective set of measures. No one can explain away anything; if results do not match up to measures, it's time for a course correction.

If you're still not convinced of the value of measures, keep this in mind: when you're measuring your efforts, you gain important self-validation that gives you encouragement and confidence to continue pressing forward.

Living Your V2MOM

When Travis and I tell colleagues about the V2MOM formula, they typically ask us how to go about making sure it actually affects the way they run their business. They point out that most organizations already have a simple mission statement that aims to chart the direction of the company. While this is certainly better than not having a mission or vision statement at all, we always reply to them that not implementing the V2MOM means missing out on an incredible opportunity to tap into your entire team's creative problem-solving power and entrepreneurial-minded spirit—an area that too often (and needlessly) goes untapped.

Benioff at Salesforce, for example, has mastered the art of bringing employees into the visioning process. He is famous in his company for providing his executive team with a broad vision and then turning it over to them to map out exactly how to make it work for themselves.[4]

Travis and I believe so strongly in the V2MOM that we prepare a separate V2MOM for ourselves that complements the company's V2MOM. We also require each member of our leadership teams to prepare their own, plus a second one for their department or division. Each of our managers, in turn, prepares a V2MOM for each of the employees he or she supervises. The end result is that every single employee has an opportunity to define how he or she will work to bring the company closer to achieving the company vision.

Part of what makes the V2MOM such a powerful tool is that it fosters a culture of accountability. Indeed, our mandate is that we make all of our V2MOMs publicly avail-

---

4 - Konrad, Alex. "Salesforce innovation secrets: How Marc Benioff's team stays on top." *Forbes Magazine*, August 20, 2014. http://www.forbes.com/sites/alexkonrad/2014/08/20/marc-benioffs-innovation-sec

able to the entire company. Without this high degree of transparency, we run the risk of devolving into an adversarial, conflict-oriented culture that demands employees live up to standards they do not believe in and don't have a say in developing.

One of the most exciting days at work for Travis and me is when we get together with our executive teams (typically about once every six months) to revisit our V2MOM and our personal V2MOMs. We value this experience so much that we often insist that we go off-site for a few days. On one particularly fun trip, I visited a professional racetrack and got behind the wheel of some high-powered muscle cars. A professional NASCAR driver helped us get up to speed, so to speak, for a whirlwind of a morning.

Although on the surface these experiences are all about just having fun with one another and building camaraderie outside the office, when we finally sit down to revisit our V2MOMs, we find that we have some of our most straightforward, frank, and heated conversations. Because we're talking about something as important as our future, this is exactly the level of dialogue we need to be having.

During the V2MOM meetings, Travis and I start by presenting our thoughts and perspectives on where the company stands in relation to the V2MOM. Then, we solicit input from the others on what they think should be removed, changed, or improved. We keep circling around the room to hear out one another and develop consensus around a V2MOM we can all support. When we're finished, we repeat the entire process for each of our personal V2MOMs and for the departmental V2MOMs.

The genius of the V2MOM process is that it empowers each individual to determine how his or her own unique talents and abilities can be used to help achieve the company vision. Along the way, those individuals experience growth, improvement, and a greater level of professional satisfaction.

As you're talking your way through this process, keep in mind that you cannot over-communicate your vision. Just because your chief operating officer spends a full fifteen minutes of your V2MOM planning meeting detailing the company vision does not mean you as the CEO cannot re-share that same vision again with everyone in the room. In fact, the more times your audience hears the vision, the more likely it is to stick—and the more likely your team is to appreciate its importance.

Finally, we want to end with this note: As hard as we try to sell our colleagues on the value of doing a V2MOM, we also recognize that a V2MOM is not the right fit for everyone. We've met folks who swear by various other approaches to fleshing out their vision. So do what works for you. All we hope is that you're convinced now of the importance of a robust, thorough visioning process.

In Sum . . .

Vision, the single most important characteristic of entrepreneurial success, starts with thinking thoroughly through what you want to achieve and using that desire to conquer self-doubting and excuses. By staying the course and guarding against our innate tendencies to avoid and delay the visioning process, you can develop a rock-solid vision through the five-part V2MOM (Vision, Values,

Methods, Obstacles, Measures). With V2MOM, you'll be empowered to live out your values, engage in productive and meaningful work methods, identify your obstacles proactively, and measure the results of these efforts in ways that help you stay on a path that ultimately leads to enviable success.

While it is easy for us to expend great energy attempting to accomplish something great on our own, it is a far more valuable skill to see through the fog and draw from others' ideas and perspectives to develop the best vision possible. "There is no limit to what a man can do or where he can go if he doesn't mind who gets the credit," reads a plaque that President Ronald Reagan once kept on his Oval Office desk.

As you work through development of your company's V2MOM, remember to take advantage of the many meaningful contributions of your employees to help you reach your company's vision. As an entrepreneur, the sooner you recognize that there is great power in other people and their ideas, the faster you will accomplish your vision— and the faster your vision will evolve and expand through the collective wisdom and insights of your employees.

ACTION PLAN

1. **Recognize that you are nowhere without a vision:** Write down an important goal you want to achieve, then outline all of the steps that you must take to achieve that goal. When your entire plan is fleshed out, you'll be looking at your vision. Without this vision, the road to success will be long, hard, and uncertain.

2. **Acknowledge that you cannot delay forming your vision:** Think about someone you know who sought to accomplish a goal without a clear, well-defined vision. Did (s)he succeed? Probably not. And that's why you need to articulate your vision from the get-go.

3. **Use the V2MOM visioning process to articulate and record a clear vision for what you want to achieve:** The visioning process has five components—vision, values, methods, obstacles, and measures—and you must flesh out each component thoroughly to set yourself on a path to success.

4. **Incorporate your V2MOM into your core business processes:** Write a V2MOM that can be integrated seamlessly into your daily workflows, one that you will intuitively find yourself thinking about as you go about your day. Set aside time at least once a year for your leadership team

to discuss your V2MOM with you and to track progress. Bring up your V2MOM in meetings and personal interactions with colleagues; the more often you talk about your V2MOM, the more often others will realize its importance and value.

5. **Encourage your leadership team to create its own V2MOMs:** Train your leadership team on how to write a V2MOM that will complement your own. Provide feedback for them and get them to provide feedback and assistance to one another. Also require them to train all subordinates on the V2MOM model and to provide time for them to write and discuss their own V2MOMs.

WORK ETHIC: THE RHYTHM OF SUCCESS

"Nothing will work unless you do."

– Maya Angelou

During the early days at my computer repair company PcCareSupport, we adopted an all-hands-on-deck mentality to keep our fledgling company afloat. Everyone from the CEO (me) to our expert repair technicians were required to step up to the plate whenever asked, often to perform menial and mundane tasks. In fact, one of my most important responsibilities in those first few months was to get in touch with customers whose credit cards had not been billed properly. Yes, our company was so small that it fell on the company's founder to spend several hours of his night on the phone, trying to resolve billing problems, one customer at a time.

Most of these customers owed us such small amounts that I questioned the time and effort I was spending. But the reality was that this thankless job was helping us to bring in just enough revenue to stay financially solvent. More importantly, it was work I could tangibly measure— a manageable, achievable responsibility that was giving me a purpose and self-confidence. And it was the type of progress that reinforced, for me, that despite all the glamour of being an entrepreneur, the ability to make my lofty dreams a reality was dependent on a lot of boring, frustrating daily tasks.

What I learned from this experience is that work ethic is about more than just working hard. It is about working hard consistently, day in and day out. It is about planning your work and then working your plan, as the saying goes. Work ethic certainly involves tremendous hard work, but it also involves smart work. Work ethic is establishing a rhythm, a cadence, a pattern of life that becomes nearly as natural as sleeping, waking, and eating.

Anyone can work hard to complete a task in record time and at a high level of quality. For example, as any high school or college student can attest, it is possible to stay up all night to write a paper or study for a test. But this is not work ethic. (It does, however, demonstrate procrastination!) A strong work ethic is so valued in our society precisely because it cannot be made overnight.

Imagine running a footrace in the backyard versus committing to become an elite, long-distance runner. One requires a short-duration burst of hard work, while the other demands sustained focus and dedication. Work ethic is always the long-distance runner, never the backyard sprint.

In this chapter, Travis and I start by explaining what our survey reveals about work ethic. Then we share with you the origins and scholarly meaning of work ethic. We also devote considerable space in this chapter to an in-depth explanation of the building blocks of institutional work ethic: the importance of delegating responsibilities, making smart hires, addressing employees with performance problems, and keeping the right focus. We close out the chapter by sharing with you how we view work ethic as its own reward, a perspective that might help you stand strong against those who try to convince you there is a way around hard, consistent work.

What Our Survey Reveals about Work Ethic

Work ethic doesn't have the star power of the other top characteristics of entrepreneurial success. In fact, most of the time, work ethic feels like a burden, reminding us that no matter how much effort we put toward achieving our goals, our progress is still likely to feel painstakingly slow.

Still, there is no question work ethic plays a critical role in business success. In our survey of business CEOs and founders, work ethic was the second most commonly cited characteristic of succeeding as an entrepreneur, picked by 45% of survey respondents.

Travis and I believe the message they were trying to send us is that "slow and steady wins the race." As one survey respondent shared with us, the formula to succeed as an entrepreneur is simple: "Work hard *and* smart."

Work ethic appears to be particularly important for businesses between two and five years old. A whopping 84% of respondents working for businesses in this age bracket picked work ethic as one of their top five characteristics of entrepreneurial success. That is in contrast to the 22% who have been in business for a year or less, and the 24% who have been in business sixteen or more years.

What CEOs and founders seem to be conveying here is that work ethic is most needed in those critical early years, when the enthusiasm and novelty of starting a business have worn off, but while the long, hard work of turning the startup into a solid, dependable business is still being accomplished.

"It's going to cost at least twice as much as you think, take twice as long, and be twice as much work as you anticipate before you start," one of our survey respondents wrote. "Be ready to work hard and stick with it day after day."

Studies of employee work ethic affirm that the early years can be a particularly trying time for a business. In one 1997 study that sought to measure the work ethic of hundreds of employees across 158 industries and businesses, workers with two to eight years of full-time work experience had lower mean scores than workers with less than two years of work experience and workers with more than eight years. The University of Georgia study concluded that young people enter the workforce with individualistic notions and a belief in the value of work but that their work ethic tends to lag as the reality of the daily grind dampens this naïve idealism. Even so, the study shows us that workers tend to regain their work ethic as they progress through their working life, especially their sense of self-initiative and dependability.[1]

What we take away from studies like this is that although work ethic may fade and diminish, it does not have to become a permanent setback. Despite whatever pressures an entrepreneur may be facing, a flagging work ethic can still come roaring back.

Overcoming the Impulse to Quit

When I was a young boy, I remember getting very excited about joining my first soccer league. At the beginning of the first season, I was enjoying the game and making new friends. It was a blast. But by the end of the season, my interest started fading; I was becoming distracted by all of the other things I thought I'd rather do instead. Although I signed up for the second season, I remember just a few games into the season telling my parents I was done with soccer. My parents were not happy. They told me that I couldn't give up in the middle of the season without a good reason; I had made a commitment to my team, and I needed to keep it. "Put in your best effort this season," they told me, "and after that, if you still want to quit, you can quit."

Although I didn't know it at the time, my parents were teaching me how to fight the natural human tendency to quit as soon as the going gets tough. And what an incredibly valuable lesson it was. Over and over in our working

---

1 · Hill, Roger B. "Demographic differences in selected work ethic attributes." *Journal of Career Development* 24.1 (1997): 3-23.

lives, Travis and I have found ourselves battling this instinctive behavior to quit.

Work ethic has its origins in the philosophy of individualism. Under this philosophy, which was conceptualized centuries ago by post-Reformation intellectuals opposed to social welfare, individuals take full responsibility for their lot in life, and it's through sustained, hard work that we improve our condition. This fierce sense of independence and self-reliance is what aided the rise of capitalism and the modern entrepreneurial mindset. In the business world, where we start with nothing and work in a sustained, concentrated manner for every dollar we earn, work ethic is the essential driver of this momentum.[2]

Unfortunately, we have seen far too many talented would-be entrepreneurs who struggle to work in a sustained, rigorous fashion. Some of them get overwhelmed and say, "Well, I just hit a ceiling. I couldn't keep going anymore." Others cannot handle the speed at which they're expected to make decisions; they get bogged down overanalyzing everything and ultimately become so frustrated that they don't want to keep going.

I once mentored an entrepreneur who was suddenly faced with a number of important decisions; his response was to study each issue for months at a time, which ultimately caused his problems to multiply and build.

What he failed to realize was that work ethic is as much about being able to take quick, decisive action when necessary as it is about working incredibly hard. The longer

---

2 - Miller, Michael J., David J. Woehr, and Natasha Hudspeth. "The meaning and measurement of work ethic: Construction and initial validation of a multidimensional inventory." *Journal of Vocational Behavior* 60.3 (2002): 451-489.

he would wait to resolve issues, the greater the financial strain he would place on himself and his company. As a company becomes more and more complex, the financial hole triggered by indecisiveness is just going to get exponentially deeper—and the desire to quit is just going to get exponentially stronger.

Dissecting Work Ethic

In Aesop's well-known fable *The Ant and the Grasshopper*, an industrious Ant works hard throughout the summer to gather supplies and materials for the long winter, while the Grasshopper spends those same summer months singing, dancing, relaxing, and having a good time. Although the Grasshopper encourages the Ant to join in the fun, the Ant refuses.

When the refreshing breezes of autumn turn to the frigid blasts of winter, the Grasshopper begs the Ant for a warm place to rest and eat. The Ant refuses, reprimanding the Grasshopper for idleness and leaving him hungry in the cold.

The story is usually told to emphasize the importance of preparing for the "winters" of life. In the modern workplace, entrepreneurs also must prepare for the "winters" of business life. But how do we know how to do the daily work that prepares us to endure through the hard times?

For starters, we can turn to an endless list of motivational quotes for an answer. They are inspiring but can only go so far in teaching us what work ethic really means.

"Genius is one percent inspiration, ninety-nine percent perspiration." -Thomas Edison

"The average person only puts twenty-five percent of his energy and ability into his work." -Andrew Carnegie

"Talent is never enough. With few exceptions, the best players are the hardest workers." -Magic Johnson

"Hard work beats talent when talent doesn't work hard." -Unknown

"I'm a great believer in luck, and I find the harder I work, the more I have of it." -Thomas Jefferson

Fortunately, work ethic is so intrinsic to our society's success that it has been extensively dissected and analyzed. We have long sought to understand the underlying psychology of what motivates people to work and how we can teach others to develop and sustain a strong work ethic.

Experts commonly refer to Americans' work ethic as the Protestant work ethic, a value system espoused by our early Christian Protestant forefathers. The Protestant work ethic was—and continues to be—so intrinsic to the American way of life that it is still extensively studied.

Perhaps our most important breakthrough on this front was the development of a scale that can scientifically measure Protestant work ethic in the modern workplace. This scale, known as the Protestant Work Ethic Scale, quantifies the level of agreement a worker has to the following series of six statements[3]:

1. Even if I won a great deal of money on the lottery, I would continue to work.

2. If unemployment benefit was really high, I would still prefer to work.

3. I would hate to live off benefits.

4. Having a job is very important to me.

5. The most important things that happen to me involve work.

6. I would soon get very bored if I had no work to do.

By pondering these statements, we're able to peer deep into the psyche of the American worker and dissect what it means to have a strong work ethic. We see that there is a wide spread of human behaviors that help us assess work ethic, ranging from a desire to not live off welfare to a fierce commitment to work even after being granted sudden financial prosperity. And we see that researchers take advantage of a series of provocative what-if scenarios to get to the core of why we work and how our lives are influenced—and even dictated—by work habits.

When it comes to entrepreneurs, of course, we don't just want to understand why and how we work. We also want to improve and hone our work ethic to optimize our chances of entrepreneurial success.

---

3 - Athayde, Rosemary. "Measuring enterprise potential in young people." *Entrepreneurship Theory and Practice* 33.2 (2009): 481-500.

Delegation: A Key to the Entrepreneurial Work Ethic

Several years ago, I had a conversation with the owner of a small car dealership. He expressed how difficult it had been for him to see significant, sustained growth for his dealership. I asked him what the problem was.

"The problem," he said, "is that I'm always the one who has to fix the cars."

"But you're the owner of the dealership, aren't you?" I replied. "Why do you have to spend so much time fixing all the cars?"

"Well, I can't find anyone who knows how to repair a transmission nearly as well as I can," he said. "I don't want my customers to receive second-rate work, so that means I have to do all the transmission work."

"You mean none of your mechanics can repair a transmission?"

"Not as well as I can."

"So your mechanics are good at everything they are asked to do, except repair transmissions?"

"Yes."

It didn't make sense. If all he was responsible for was one specific type of job, why was his business in so much trouble? I probed him further.

"So you're telling me that the only thing you don't trust your mechanics to do on their own is repair transmissions? There's nothing else that you make sure to take care of on your own?"

He fidgeted for a second, then said, "Well, we also sell rebuilt titles because we're able to make more in the margins. The problem is that it takes five weeks to finish the repairs."

"Five weeks? That seems like a long time. Why does it take so long?"

"Because I'm the only one who can do it right."

The other ball had dropped, and it was quite telling. I didn't want to embarrass him, but I probably could have continued my line of questioning and heard more of the same. No matter how talented his employees might be, this business owner was convinced that no one was as talented as he.

The saddest part of this exchange is that both Travis and I have heard this story time and again. Entrepreneurs from all industries and backgrounds outwardly project confidence in their own abilities, but inwardly are terrified about sharing responsibility with others. And this, of course, is the polar opposite of confidence.

The excuses that these entrepreneurs give fall into a few main categories. It's important to be aware of them and how easy it is to fall into their trap, so we want to walk you through them one by one:

1. Inexperienced entrepreneurs refuse to delegate to employees and other subordinates because they might prove to do a better job than their boss.

This may sound like a reasonable statement to us at first blush. No business founder wants to see the rug pulled out from under him, to lose everything to someone who was once a trusted confidant. But this is all hogwash. Successful entrepreneurs recognize that the road to business success cannot be traveled alone. We must learn to trust others to build something great. Travis and I believe that if we are the smartest folks in the room, then we are in the wrong room. To be a successful leader, it is absolutely essential for you to recognize that, no matter how intelligent or talented you are, there is always somebody who is smarter, more gifted, and more experienced than you. And this is not a bad thing; after all, it's far better for these talented people to be your employees than your competitors.

In the dog-eat-dog world of free enterprise, there is too much at stake to let personal insecurities stand in the way of long-term prosperity. If one of your mechanics has the potential to repair a car's transmission better than you, there's no reason not to turn over this responsibility to him. And if you're struggling to find someone who can repair transmissions as well as you can, you need to train your employees better or hire somebody new. Either way, a bet on your employees is the smartest bet you can make.

2. Inexperienced entrepreneurs insist that training employees to do their work for them would take far more time and effort than doing it themselves.

When business leaders tell me or Travis that training their employees requires too much time, we are always baffled. Our experience suggests that there isn't enough time not to provide better training for employees. There is a good reason for the saying, "An ounce of prevention is worth a pound of cure." In the long run, entrepreneurs can only expect to find long-term, sustained success for their businesses when they train their employees to be proactive, free agents capable of performing important tasks and solving common problems on their own. A few hours or a few days or even a few weeks of training are worth far more than the never-ending responsibility of doing something on your own.

3. Inexperienced entrepreneurs decide that because the buck stops with them, they must personally supervise, manage, and correct virtually everything their employees do—in other words, they micromanage.

Entrepreneurs generally understand that they need to delegate some of their responsibilities because, if nothing else, it creates the appearance they're doing their jobs properly. The problem is that inexperienced leaders will check up on those same employees almost as soon as the assignments are doled out to make sure they are being fulfilled in precisely the way the leader would have done them. But that is micromanagement, not delegation. True delegation involves assigning responsibility for solving a problem or performing a task to someone else. When an employee is micromanaged, he doesn't have real responsibility to think through the problem on his own, make an informed decision about how best to solve that problem, and use his own resources to solve the problem.

Furthermore, it's only through meaningful delegation that entrepreneurs can carve out enough time and attention to maintain focus on their vision. In fact, when workers are empowered to use their own knowledge, skills, experience, wisdom, and creativity to solve problems, their employer is far more likely to find more long-term solutions to a bigger range of problems.

Across all of these entrepreneurial shortcomings, the solution is always to find qualified employees with a strong work ethic who can step up to the plate. But how do we hire the right people to fill this critically important gap? We can start by pinpointing exactly what gaps we need filled.

Build Work Ethic by Hiring the Right People

Every once in a while, Travis and I come across an entrepreneur who, in a self-imposed rush to add manpower, hires employees fairly indiscriminately. This type of business leader is convinced there are really only a few positions in the company that deserve strict scrutiny; the rest can be filled by friends, family, or the first smiling face who walks through the office door. But the reality is that every employee makes a huge difference in building a strong institutional work ethic. In fact, one bad apple can quickly poison the whole barrel.

This is why entrepreneurs must do everything they can to make smart hiring decisions. Especially in the early, formative stages of a company's growth, the candidates for employment should have three core qualifications: they must be right for the job, right for your business culture, and right for achieving your vision. Let's explore each of these in detail.

1. Right for the job

Generally speaking, you want to hire people who already have at least some experience in the field in which they're applying to work. If you are hiring an accountant, you need to make sure all of the candidates you interview are, at minimum, certified accountants. If you own a logging business, you need to make sure all of your employees, regardless of job classification, are comfortable working in the presence of heavy, dangerous machinery. Although this might seem like an obvious step, Travis and I are continually surprised by the number of entrepreneurs who don't develop a distinct picture in their minds of who they need to hire until after they've begun the interview process. We're not saying that every job candidate needs to have years of relevant work experience, of course, but you need to decide how much work experience is needed before you start the hiring process.

Early in my career, after being promoted to a sales manager position, I found myself leading people with no prior sales experience. They were bright, motivated individuals who had come from jobs in landscaping, concrete laying, car washing, and other skilled trades. Although they might not have had the track record to demonstrate that they were exceptional salespeople, many of these folks ended up being among our company's top sales leaders—the type of people who proved to me that, when given the chance, it is possible to overcome inexperience and shine.

2. Right for your business culture

Because so many factors make up a company's business culture—people, industry, leadership, vision, location, and so forth—not every person who is qualified for a job on paper is actually going to be the right fit for your company. The best way to draw this out is during the interview process, when you can ask candidates all about the business culture at their past jobs. What hours are they accustomed to working? What kind of friendships did they develop with coworkers? What do they expect out of the work environment? What kind of dress code, if any, did they have? To elicit meaningful responses, you want to not only tell them about your own company culture, but also show them around your office so they can see firsthand what a typical day at your office looks like. And when they ask you questions about company culture, it's important to answer them in the most honest, straightforward way you can.

Interestingly, what Travis and I have found is that candidates who realize they won't be a good fit for your company culture often remove themselves from consideration on their own. Conversely, those who are convinced they will mesh well will be eager to share this information.

3. Right for achieving your vision

The employees who are right for helping you achieve your vision need to have three elements: They must be passionate about your business, they must bring something new to the table, and they must be smarter than you in at least one respect. Too many entrepreneurs make the mistake of believing that their employees don't need to have nearly the same level of passion for the business as they do. "It is my job to care passionately about my business," they say, "and it is my employees' job to do what I pay them to do." But they're doing themselves, their company, and their customers a great disservice. For example, let's say you run a tech support company. Your goal should be to hire people who are as passionate as you are about helping customers to solve problems with their computers; you don't want someone who merely feels they're getting a paycheck to do this work.

You also want to hire someone who brings something new to the table—a skill, a talent, a type of experience that can't be found among your employee ranks—that will help you move closer to achieving your vision. Finally, you want to hire someone who is smarter than you because, if for no other reason, you don't want them to end up as your competitor.

The secret to hiring smart is a transparent, in-depth interview process where you can really vet your candidates. Don't shy away from telling job candidates what your company is, what it stands for, and what its vision is. Your goal should be to maximize the chances that both the interviewer and the interviewee walk away from the interview having ascertained whether this candidate is going to complement or hurt your company's work ethic.

Addressing Poor Work Ethic

Even when we go to great lengths to make sure the people we hire are right for the job, right for our corporate culture, and right for achieving our vision, people change for the worse. There are all sorts of reasons that employees' work ethics can falter. Among the commonly cited reasons are souring relationships between management and labor, family instability, drug problems, changes to economic policies that impact the industry in which the employee works, and loss of confidence in the organization itself. Contrary to what many believe, these changes don't cause an employee to become lazy and unmotivated; rather, they lead to employee alienation.[4]

Fortunately, in many instances, you can avoid firing underperforming employees by working with them to create a plan for getting back on track. Sometimes all it takes is a frank discussion of the personal issues they're grappling with, followed by outlining some fair but unmistakable benchmarks that must be met to get the employee back on track.

During this time, it's important to set clear guidelines and be honest about the potential consequences of failure to live up to those guidelines and reach agreed-upon benchmarks. It is also important to maintain regular, personal contact with the employee. Many entrepreneurs tend to avoid underperforming employees altogether for days, weeks, even months, in the unrealistic hope that a problem will correct itself. "Maybe if I just leave him or her alone for a while," they convince themselves, "the problem will take care of itself." But work ethic is not always a self-correcting phenomenon. In fact, employees who lose their work ethic become less likely to want to confront problems on their own.

Sometimes, despite your best efforts to help struggling employees improve, you have no choice but to separate them from the company. Business leaders from all walks of life say that firing people is one of the most unpleasant aspects of leadership, and that is particularly true of entrepreneurs who run startups. Not only are small startups often desperate for whatever help they can get their hands

---

4 - Ali, Abbas J., Thomas Falcone, and Ahmed A. Azim. "Work ethic in the USA and Canada." *Journal of Management Development* 14.6 (1995): 26-34.

on, but many of them are run by young, inexperienced entrepreneurs who don't have the foresight to know when a personnel-related situation isn't going to get better.

As unpleasant and distasteful as it is to fire someone, it is never worse for you than for the employee being fired. So be kind, compassionate, direct, honest, and brief. And remember not to lose sight of the big picture. To achieve your vision, you need to delicately but proactively get rid of anything and anyone standing in your way.

Once you've cleared these obstacles, you'll be able to maintain a relentless, razor-like focus on the things that matter. The right things.

Build Work Ethic by Focusing on the Right Things

Not long after getting one of my early businesses up and running, I began to see a number of encouraging signs that seemed to suggest that I should expand our business services division. I knew it was a very risky idea, but the forces urging us to grow geographically seemed too great at the time.

We decided to open a satellite office in Dallas, more than 1,200 miles from our Utah headquarters. We were so confident in the Dallas experiment that we even relocated one of our employees and his family there. At first, the signs were all positive. But several months later, the good news dried up, and it became painfully evident the Dallas office was a mistake.

What did we do wrong? In a nutshell, we lost sight of our vision to be an industry leader in Utah's booming tech sector. Dallas was a shiny distraction for us; it was attractive precisely because it was a distraction. Dallas did not fit into our strategic master plan at all, and once we were able to admit this, we were finally able to bring ourselves to close down the office and return to focusing on the core service market in Utah.

Once we were back on track, we realized we had barely begun to scratch the surface of our master vision; indeed, there was still a lot of market share in Utah we were not even aware we hadn't tapped into yet. Although we ultimately built the business services division of the company into a thriving unit focused on the Utah market, we felt the financial reverberations of our ill-advised Dallas office for years to come—and all because we lost focus of our vision.

Experiences like the Dallas experiment are unfortunately remarkably common among entrepreneurs. By nature, we are willing to take on a lot of risks. These risks present incredible opportunities for us to demonstrate our unfailing focus and determination, but we cannot succeed at everything—and thus we run the risk of never achieving our vision.

The problem is that there is a fine line between work ethic and work-aholism. Those who take the time to develop a vision—and then stay focused on that vision, even as incredibly attractive and lucrative distractions come their way—are the ones with strong work ethic. If you're not staying focused, you're probably just a workaholic.

Few people have had a greater impact on how I think about the importance of maintaining focus than Jim Collins, author of the bestselling book *Good to Great*. Collins researched dozens of the world's elite companies to understand how good companies, mediocre companies, and even bad companies can achieve enduring success. One of his most important revelations is what he calls the "hedgehog concept"—the idea that the most visionary entrepreneurs are simple creatures (hedgehogs) who are good at only one thing, while less successful entrepreneurs are clever, crafty animals (foxes) who can do many things well. Although foxes intuitively sound like they will make better leaders, Collins argues that foxes are so good at doing so many different things that they are unable to focus their energy around a single, visionary idea.[5]

"Foxes pursue many ends at the same time and see the world in all its complexity," writes Collins, who explains that his analogy was inspired by Isaiah Berlin's famous essay on splitting the world's population into two categories—hedgehogs and foxes.

Collins notes Berlin's theory that foxes are "'scattered or diffused, moving on many levels,' . . . never integrating their thinking into one overall concept or unifying vision." Hedgehogs, meanwhile, simplify a complex world into a basic principle that unifies and guides everything. It "doesn't matter how complex the world; a hedgehog reduces all challenges and dilemmas to simple—indeed, almost simplistic—hedgehog ideas. For a hedgehog, anything that does not somehow relate to the hedgehog's idea holds no relevance."

Collins's conclusion is that once a truly successful entrepreneur has his visionary "hedgehog idea" firmly

---

5 - Collins, Jim, *Good to Great: Why Some Companies Make the Leap . . . and Others Don't*. (New York: HarperBusiness, 2001), p. 91.

planted in his head, he will have the clairvoyance to view every other competing vision as a distraction that is not worthy of his energy or time.

Travis and I absolutely agree that it's the hedgehogs who are best poised for sustained success. Foxes, despite their immense talents, are constantly fighting their innate tendency to spread themselves too thinly.

A wise CEO once told me, "All I do is recruit the most talented people, raise money, and drive strategy. I'm not involved in the day-to-day operation of the business at all." His reasoning is simple. He knows it is far too easy to become distracted by venturing down into the weeds.

Successful entrepreneurs understand that maintaining a singular focus on vision is not about simply preparing a fancy-looking document and referring to it once a year in company-wide, year-in-review meetings. Rather, maintaining a focus at the hedgehog level is the most important job they can do—a seemingly simple job that is, at its core, a powerful show of work ethic.

Work Ethic Is Its Own Reward

I spent several years of my childhood working with my grandfather on a farm. We would wake up early in the morning, well before dawn, to accomplish everything we needed to get done each day.

Our daily tasks included throwing huge bales of hay into trucks, filling grain silos, feeding cows and chickens, repairing fence posts, and chopping down corn stalks. I grew up believing the only way to live life was to do this difficult work every day. The longer I worked on the farm, the more I came to appreciate how gratifying it is to work patiently on something for a long time, see the rewards of that work, and be motivated by those rewards to keep working harder.

This is why Travis and I view work ethic as a reward in and of itself. When we're working hard on something meaningful and are able to start seeing the results of our work, we experience a huge boost of morale. Even though our particular task might seem like unbearable drudgery–for example, verifying that customer credit cards were properly billed, or figuring out the single error in a fifty-page accounting ledger–hard work propels us and lifts our spirits. Hard work reminds us that even if our vision will not fully be realized for a long time, the progress we're making is going to be well worth our while.

This attitude is especially important to adopt in the entrepreneurial world, where we cannot expect that the most desirable rewards will come to us easily, and where we're often called upon to perform tasks outside of our comfort zone that seem beneath us.

When Travis was working as CEO of an Internet service provider, he received a message on his phone one Christmas morning about a major tower that had just gone down, disrupting Internet service to hundreds of his customers. The tower was a three-hour drive from Travis's home, and Travis couldn't find anyone to go fix the tower (it was Christmas Day, after all). Travis could have left his customers stranded without Internet service for the day, but Travis knew that all of his customers would be at home on Christmas Day counting on their Internet service to entertain and connect them to the outside world.

So he did what he had to do. He drove out to the tower and repaired it himself, abandoning his own family for more than eight hours in the process. It was a sacrifice he made without question.

Unfortunately, Travis and I are always amazed that hard work does not inspire and drive the work ethic of all entrepreneurs.

Take the number of "entrepreneurs" who choose an entrepreneurial career path because they're convinced they'll be able to spend more time playing golf than in the office. The notion of a four-hour work week—espoused by some self-proclaimed entrepreneurs as a point of pride—is particularly mind-boggling to us.

Just as there is no such thing as a "get rich quick" scheme, so, too, is there no such thing as a "get rich without a work ethic" scheme.

Religious leader and former Brigham Young University president Jeffrey R. Holland framed the value of a strong work ethic in rather stark terms when he said, "Surely fluttering somewhere over the highway to hell is the local chamber-of-horrors banner reading, 'Welcome to the ethics of ease.'"[6]

He's absolutely right, of course. Far too many people pay lip service to the virtues of work ethic, and far too few are willing to put those virtues into practice.

Final Thoughts on Work Ethic

Some people seem to have an almost natural ability to

6 - Holland, Jeffrey R., "The Inconvenient Messiah." Brigham Young University devotional address, February 15, 1982. http://www.speeches.byu.edu, accessed August 4, 2014.

put their heads down and go to work on something until it is done. But for most people, developing good work ethic can seem like an impossibly difficult uphill battle. There are far more people who fall into the latter group.

The fact is that no one can truly transform his or her work ethic overnight. At the same time, it is possible to take steps to stay in the proper mindset.

Start by spending a few minutes thinking about something in your professional or personal life that needs to be done but that you have avoided doing. Perhaps it will be a big project that could take many months.

Write it down on a sticky note and set a goal for when it should be complete. Then, place it somewhere you will see every day, such as the bathroom mirror or on your keyboard at work. At the end of each day, ask yourself this simple question: "What work did I do today to bring myself closer to achieving my goal?" You might even start keeping a notebook or journal to track your progress.

What you'll gradually realize is that in three months or six months or a year, your incremental, consistent steps made it possible for you to achieve your goal.

As an entrepreneurial leader, your job is to work proactively to improve and maintain work ethic. One of the best ways you can do this is by making your company vision clear and ensuring your employees believe in it. When your employees believe in the big-picture goals of what you all are collectively trying to achieve, they're more likely to work harder, smarter, and in a more disciplined fashion.

The value of consistency and moderation in work cannot be overstated. In fact, researchers who have studied entrepreneurial work ethic say that impulsive, overzealous bursts of work will get you nowhere. That's because one of two things starts happening: we surpass our tolerance threshold for work and start to break down, or we start sacrificing the long-term rewards we're working toward for more immediate, less strategic gain.[7]

Interestingly, even as you get better at honing your work ethic, what you'll realize is that the people around you won't recognize it. Instead, they're likely to tell you how lucky you got. Travis and I cannot count the number of times we've shared some of our most difficult, hard-won success stories, only to have folks respond with, "Wow, you got very lucky."

We understand we don't work hard to be validated by our peers during small talk at happy hour, but it's certainly troubling—and telling—that so many people don't appreciate the role that a strong work ethic plays in entrepreneurial success.

As we survey the business landscape and think about many of the great men and women who have come before us, we cannot identify a single person who has made it—who has been successful and stayed successful—without putting in a tremendous amount of hard work. We have never once heard a successful person say, "Gosh, that hardly required any work at all. I was really lazy for a long time and built a billion-dollar business." Not once.

We have heard the opposite many times. And more importantly, we have seen the rewards of hard work first-

---

7 - Porter, Gayle. "Work, work ethic, work excess." *Journal of Organizational Change Management* 17.5 (2004): 424-439.

hand. The truth is that any of us can be successful if we want it badly enough and know how to channel our energy—into a healthy, strong, consistent work ethic.

In Sum . . .

Work ethic is a critical part of entrepreneurial success, of the daily rhythm by which we stay focused, engaged and committed to the work that gets us to where we want to be. As entrepreneurs, we can improve the institutional work ethic at our businesses by delegating responsibilities appropriately, making smart hires, addressing employees with performance problems, and keeping the right focus. We also can improve our focus by learning to view work ethic as its own reward; this becomes especially critical when we become convinced there might be an easy way around hard, consistent work.

When I cofounded the tech support company PcCare-Support several years ago, we started on a shoestring budget. Because we had no budget for marketing, we got out the word the old-fashioned way: knocking on doors, hand-delivering fliers and business cards, cold-calling, and asking for referrals.

ACTION PLAN

1. **Understand that work ethic is more than just working hard:** Ask yourself if you work in marathon sprints (followed by burnout) or if you work incrementally and steadily. If your answer is the former, it's important to recognize there's room for improvement to your work ethic. Work ethic is about sustained, hard work every day.

2. **Recognize and learn to fight the innate tendency to give up:** Think back to the moments when you've felt overwhelmed and stressed. What was it about those moments that made you feel like giving up? By recognizing which situations trigger this weakness, you can be cognizant of when you should be fighting the hardest to keep going.

3. **Study the Protestant Work Ethic:** The Protestant Work Ethic is the foundation of the modern American work ethic. By understanding how we view and relate to work, we can understand how to improve our own work ethic and how to enhance it in others.

4. **Learn how to delegate responsibilities:** Make a list of all of your daily responsibilities, then ask yourself if you're truly the only employee at your company who could do those tasks. Almost everything that we, as entrepreneurs, feel compelled to do could and should be done by

others. The key to entrepreneurial success is to leave these tasks to others and to focus your attention on the big picture.

5. **Implement a best-practices approach to hiring the right people:** Establish outcome-oriented goals for every candidate you interview, then design an interview experience to achieve those goals. Design interview questions in advance to ensure you extract key pieces of information from the. candidate. Craft talking points that ensure you're effectively communicating to your prospective employee what your company is all about.

6. **Take a firm stand against the poor work ethic of others:** Institute an objective way to measure your employees' work ethic. If they come up short, you'll know when you need to intervene to correct the behavior and, if it continues, when to separate the employee from your company.

RESILIENCE: THE SECRET SAUCE OF SUCCESS

"Many of life's failures are people who did not realize how close they were to success when they gave up."

— *Thomas Edison*

During those first few months, none of those strategies were working. We were barely growing, and I began to question whether we'd survive. Despite working very hard to execute a rock-solid business plan with a clear vision, we had almost nothing to show for it. It was a difficult, frustrating, depressing situation for my team.

Gradually, my leadership team began to come to terms with the fact that it might be an appropriate time to throw in the towel and cut our losses. In fact, one of the four cofounders did just that.

My assessment of the situation was that our problems stemmed from the lack of a marketing budget. We couldn't grow fast enough; we couldn't even turn enough of a profit to be able to issue paychecks to the three remaining founders.

But I was determined to try to make this work. I organized a strategic planning session that started, as so many had before, on a depressing note. We lamented the fact that we couldn't grow without a marketing budget, and yet without growth, we could never afford a bigger marketing budget. It was a classic catch-22 situation.

Still, I wasn't about to let this strategic planning session end with a whimper. Yes, all of our marketing methods had failed to date, and yes, we still had no budget to buy marketing or advertising spaces. What we did have, though, was expertise repairing computers. What if the solution didn't involve any money at all, but, rather, an exchange of computer repair services for advertising services?

It was the lightbulb moment our team needed. We decided we would reach out to several local radio stations and ask them to run PcCareSupport advertisements in exchange for us servicing their computer networks. Perhaps the idea seems like a no-brainer in retrospect, but it was a game-changer for our tired, brain-fried team.

To our delight, a radio station that needed a major upgrade to its networks took the bite. We put all of our focus and energy on this deal. We believed it would bring us a huge pool of new customers and would save our company.

The phone didn't start ringing off the hook after the first radio ad aired. In fact, even after all of our ads had aired, we never generated the volume of sales leads we were looking for. But this experience marked a turning point for us. We were no longer letting the obstacles in our path beat us down and force us to give up. We were demonstrating resilience.

Resilience is not about maintaining a path forward in spite of our obstacles, but, rather, because of them. Resilience is the secret sauce of success because it presents us with obstacles that become our opportunities to learn, grow, develop, and thrive. Travis and I believe that if we avoid our obstacles—even if we're fortunate enough to find success anyway—we don't truly progress and grow. As the saying goes, "Don't pray for a lighter load, but for a stronger back."

This is the essence of resiliency. A resilient person recognizes that difficulties are simply part of life and that attempts to avoid these difficulties are as futile as they are short-sighted. A resilient person embraces obstacles as opportunities for growth and learning—and emerges with a wealth of wisdom and experience for it.

Academic studies of entrepreneurial success have shown that there is a predictive relationship between resilience and company growth. One recent five-year study of entrepreneurs in the tourism industry, for example, found that entrepreneurs who are able to demonstrate resilience are more likely to see their businesses grow and prosper.[1]

In this chapter on resilience, we start by digging down deep into what the data from our survey tells us about the importance of entrepreneurial resilience. Then we discuss

1 - Ayala, Juan-Carlos, and Manzano Guadalupe. The Resilience of the Entrepreneur: Influence on the Success of the Business - A Longitudinal Analysis. *Journal of Economic Psychology.* 6 (2014): 42.

the inherent value of opposition and explore the numerous incorrect ways that we tend to respond to opposition. We also explore the two main factors that we believe are eroding resilience: society's instant-gratification mindset and a tendency to dodge accountability. We close out the chapter by looking at how to identify the limitations of resilience and how resilience, when applied correctly, can lead to great rewards.

We'll also return at the end of this chapter to my PcCareSupport radio ad campaign, which, in a very roundabout and unexpected way, paid off more handsomely than I ever could have hoped.

What Our Survey Reveals about Resilience

Resilience was the third most commonly chosen characteristic of entrepreneurial success, selected by 42% of the 2,631 business CEOs and founders who responded to our survey. Respondents recognized that resilience is the only viable road for entrepreneurs and that without resilience, we cannot learn and grow.

"Entrepreneurs need to understand that the road to success is a tough one," one survey respondent shared with us. "You may have the best idea in the world, but you need the resolve to stay the course to see your idea through to fruition, even in the face of the biggest challenges imaginable."

Psychologists who have studied resilience say that this character trait is formed through a combination of hope, optimism, and confidence. Research has shown that people who possess these three factors are more likely to bounce back from adversity than those who do not.[2]

Because resilience is a characteristic that must be sustained over the life of a business—and, indeed, over the life of an entrepreneur—we were particularly interested in using the data to understand how perceptions of the value of resilience change over time.

Not surprisingly, the spread was dramatic. The respondents most likely to select resilience were those who have been in business two to five years. A whopping 80% of them identified resilience as one of the top five characteristics of entrepreneurial success.

The longer the respondent had been in business, the less likely they were to select resilience. Among those in business for six to ten years, 41% of respondents selected resilience. In the eleven- to fifteen-year bracket, 35% of respondents chose resilience.

What I take away from this is that the first five years represent the make-or-break years, when resilience is viewed as essential to building a foundation for long-term success. If an entrepreneur can't demonstrate unabashed resilience in those first five years, the reality is the business won't make it.

As one of our survey respondents put it so succinctly, "Failure is an option. Learn from the mistake/failure, and go at it again."

And that is really the value of resilience; it recognizes that obstacles and failures are an integral part of the path to entrepreneurial success.

---

2 - Luthans, F., Vogelgesang, G.R., & Lester, P.B. 2006. Developing the psychological capital of resiliency. *Human Resource Development Review*, 5.1: 25-44.

The Inherent Value of Opposition

My love of basketball as a child—and the uphill battle I faced in order to play—provided me with one of my earliest lessons about resilience and how opposition shapes and fosters resilience.

Growing up in the Philadelphia suburb of Bensalem in the early 1990s, I wanted nothing more than to join an organized league to hone my skill. My friends in elementary school were all enrolled in fee-based city leagues, but my father was a financially struggling college student at the time, and our family simply could not afford the price tag for me to join a league. As I watched my friends improve their jump shots, passes, and pivots under the expert guidance of skilled coaches, my childhood self could not help but feel dejected. Although I could play basketball by myself, I didn't feel I would ever get to the level I wanted on my own.

When I was eight, my parents moved to Utah, and I finally got to enroll in my first organized league. It quickly became painfully obvious I had some major catching up to do. During my first season, I scored a total of fourteen points—and that includes the basket I accidentally scored on the opponents' hoop!

My teammates openly mocked me, calling me Steve Young. (This might be a great compliment as a football player, but in basketball, it's anything but complimentary.) I left that season completely crushed. I realized that I hadn't simply fallen behind the curve because I was late to join a league; I was just a terrible basketball player.

Had I not cared about basketball so much, I probably would have never set foot on a court again. But I did care. I cared because I loved basketball, and I dreamed all my life of being a great basketball player. I desperately wanted to prove to all of my teammates I could be every bit as good as them. I resolved then and there that when we reached middle school basketball tryouts, I would show up, and I would make the cut.

For the next few years, I played basketball morning, noon, and night. My parents installed a halogen light on our driveway so I could continue practicing late into the night. They had to call me in almost nightly to tell me it was time for bed. I also invited over my teammates who teased me mercilessly about my performance on the court.

As I expected, most of the time I lost these one-on-one battles. But with time, I developed new skills, learned solid strategies, and started visualizing game-time plays in my head.

When basketball tryouts day finally arrived in the seventh grade, I was overwhelmed. Almost 300 players showed up. My years of intense work, dedication, and practice were all converging on this moment.

I played my hardest, and in the end my hard work paid off. I made the team, albeit as the alternate eleventh player on a team of ten. For some players, it would have been a disappointment to have just missed being named one of the ten. But I couldn't have been more thrilled to be named the sole alternate. This small achievement marked a big win for me, a reminder that even in the face of overwhelming obstacles that had dogged me for much of my childhood, I could emerge victorious.

I firmly believe that resilience is a character trait we develop and hone through obstacles and adversity. Although I always felt like an underdog in basketball—perpetually less prepared and less skilled than my teammates—resilience is what kept me going all those long nights shooting hoops by myself. Likewise, when my seventh grade tryouts put me up against guys who were bigger than me, stronger than me, faster than me, and more talented than me, I relied on resilience to stay the course and play my best. I made the team by working harder than anyone else and by giving a performance that, while not all-star, was a shining example of exceptional discipline and dedication.

As adults, Travis and I have realized that opposition comes in all forms. Take founding partners, for example. Partners are huge assets when you are starting a company. They can help with the workload and the financial startup costs, and they can be counted on to invest deeply in the company's success. They also help keep everyone motivated and working hard.

But sometimes, your company will outgrow a partner. Having to force out one of your own partners—the folks who helped build your company into what it is today—can be hugely heartbreaking and one of the most difficult things you'll ever have to do. It's emotionally draining, and the loss of someone at the top can trigger a domino effect of organizational realignments. Still, this obstacle is something that must be overcome to keep your business viable over the long run.

We've since come to realize there are a number of wrong ways to look at the obstacles in our path. Travis and I have been fortunate to consistently choose the right way.

In business, however, we're the first to acknowledge it can be easy to give in to the wrong way.

The Wrong Ways to View Opposition

It is simply a truth of human existence that there is an opposition in all things. In business, there are obstacles and setbacks you *will* face. As an entrepreneur, we can choose to look at this opposition the wrong way or the right way. Unfortunately, many entrepreneurs don't view opposition through the right lens. These flawed ways of thinking fall into three main categories.

The Entrepreneur of Convenience

Some entrepreneurs hold preconceived notions that certain forms of opposition are insurmountable and not even worth trying to overcome. These are the entrepreneurs who will only go as far as convenience and their comfort zone will take them. When Christopher Columbus set sail in search of a new trade route to India, naysayers had already drawn up maps that assigned an ominous label to the place he was headed: "Here be dragons."[3] The prevailing mentality at the time prevented them from even fathoming that someone could survive a voyage due west.

The Entrepreneur of Control

Some entrepreneurs get derailed when they begin to view opposition as a sign they're losing control of their own destiny. It's not that the task they are attempting to accomplish is impossible, they argue, but rather that external

---

3 · Warner, Marina. *World of Myths*, Volume 1 (Austin: University of Texas Press, 2013).

forces are taking away their control. In business, this type of entrepreneur refuses to take ownership of problems, arguing that responsibility for devising solutions falls to someone or something else (assuming the problems can be fixed at all).

The Entrepreneur of Destruction

Some entrepreneurs view opposition as an annoyance and a distraction that needs to be obliterated for them to achieve their vision. They don't see obstacles as opportunities to teach us anything or to help us refocus our problem-solving abilities.

If Travis and I were to rank these flawed ways of looking at opposition, we would say that the entrepreneur of convenience is the most flawed; these folks won't even leave their pre-defined comfort zones. The entrepreneur of destruction, we would argue, is the least flawed; at least these folks are going full throttle, even if they aren't learning anything along the way.

But ranking these flaws doesn't get to the heart of why well-intentioned entrepreneurs look at obstacles the wrong way. We believe the roots of these misguided thought processes can be found in the development of our modern society—and, specifically, in the viral spread of our instant-gratification mindset.

Instant Gratification Erodes Resilience

Spending my formative years living on a farm in Utah, I experienced firsthand the necessity of patience in reaping the rewards of hard work. When we planted seeds in May, we couldn't harvest crops the next day or the next month;

we had to wait until the fall. And even then, we still could be occasionally delayed by forces beyond our control. A dry spell might set us back from harvesting our crops, or a broken piece of farm equipment might put us into a holding pattern until we could get it fixed. No matter what obstacles we faced, we needed patience to push forward, find solutions to our problems, and learn from our experiences. Indeed, this is the very essence of resilience.

Today, very few among us have ever experienced the joys (and frustrations) of growing our own food. Think about the last time you breezed through your local drive-thru ordering a meal to go. You might have spent five minutes ordering, paying, and retrieving your food—all through the open window of your car door.

The reality, of course, is that it takes far more time for that food to be ready for us to consume. To produce something as common as a hamburger, there are cattle to be raised, grains to be grown, tomatoes to be planted, lettuce to be cultivated, cucumbers to be pickled, onions to be grown, ketchup and mustard to be manufactured, buns to be baked—you get the idea. Any one of these steps takes months or years to make happen, but in our modern world, the production of our hamburger seems to start when we place an order and ends when we eagerly unwrap it a few moments later.

As with food production, the last few hundred years of human history have witnessed gargantuan leaps in our ability to tame most of the earth's natural obstacles to human progress. Not only have technological advancements eliminated or dramatically simplified many of our everyday chores, but they have also made it possible for us to obtain virtually anything we want—with virtually no patience required. From music to movies to travel to communication to food to relationships, any person can have just about anything they desire almost instantaneously.

There's no question that technological advancements have enriched our lives and made it possible for people to focus on solving more high-level tasks. But as good as technological advancement has been for society, it has also ushered in generations of humanity that cannot appreciate the value of delaying gratification to achieve more meaningful, long-term rewards.[4] Many entrepreneurs seem to believe that being patient involves sitting back and waiting for the good tidings to flow to them. While patience certainly necessitates waiting, waiting is only a small part of patience. Patience means being willing to make a relatively small payment now to fully experience the rewards of that payment later, all the while working diligently to ensure that those long-term rewards will be realized. It involves intentionally delaying gratification to attain a more meaningful, realized gratification. You will never hear a truly patient entrepreneur say, "I can wait because it's not essential to my success." The patient entrepreneur says, "I will wait because I care deeply about what I am trying to do. I may not reach my goals immediately, but I will continue to work toward accomplishing them."

The most important time to exercise resilience is not when it's easy to be patient, but when we are impatient—that is, when we feel we've already worked long and hard enough to deserve to have our goals realized. Travis and I

---

4 - Seaward, Brian. *Managing Stress: A Creative Journal* (Burlington, MA: Jones & Bartlett Learning, 2011).

have seen far too many talented entrepreneurs with promise and potential fail to be patient when it matters the most. They become frustrated that they have not become as successful as soon as they thought and throw their hands in the air, declaring that the goals that once inspired them to work for greatness simply cannot be achieved. The tragedy is that most of the time, business leaders who reach such conclusions are much closer to reaching their goals than they believe.

Our expectation of instant gratification isn't the only reason we struggle with resilience. As a society, we also have a tough time holding ourselves accountable when things go wrong for us—or, at least, not as well as we had planned. And that philosophy permeates the world of entrepreneurship.

Travis and I have come to realize that the accountability we impose upon ourselves is a key reason we've found some measure of success. Although we've had plenty of opportunities to make excuses and blame circumstances outside our control, we did not let them get the better of us.

Lack of Accountability Erodes Resilience

Early in my career, while reviewing the performance of one of my employees, I began to notice a consistent theme in how he discussed his own work. Although he acknowledged generally failing to produce satisfactory results, he wasn't willing to take the blame for any of his failures. As I sat across from him listening to what amounted to an hour's worth of excuses, all I could think about was how, in the time he spent coming up with elaborate excuses for his failures, he could have solved many of his problems two or three times over. Although I had to bite my tongue, I wanted to just tell him, "It has got to be totally exhausting for you to put in such an impressive amount of effort coming up with such epic excuses. Wouldn't it have been so much easier for you to just devise a solution?"

In an effort to avoid accountability, such finger-pointing is depressingly common in workplaces everywhere. Travis and I have observed that the entrepreneurs who deflect blame fall into two main groups: those who argue that something was beyond their control and those who define their responsibilities so narrowly that they can absolve themselves of blame.

The more cancerous of these arguments makes the case that obstacles are the result of factors beyond our reach, which is extremely seductive, largely because it sounds so reasonable. After all, no one can blame you if your failures stemmed from issues you couldn't control, right? In fact, this argument sounds so appealing that you can easily convince yourself you deserve to be off the hook.

The other main way that entrepreneurs avoid accountability is to narrowly define the scope of their responsibilities. Not coincidentally, they often create a too-narrow vision to match. Armed with this argument, they do only what they feel is necessary and respond to their shortcomings with phrases like, "That's not my job," and "I can only do so much."

Travis and I cringe when we hear entrepreneurs talking like this. A true entrepreneur actively seeks to hold himself accountable for every facet of his business, especially the responsibilities that aren't obviously tied to him.

No matter how entrepreneurs try to duck accountability, the end result is reduced resilience. And that's a shame, because the only way we can learn resilience is when, in the face of overwhelming obstacles, we take ownership of these obstacles and recognize we have the power to solve them.

How to Build Resilience

Vince Lombardi, the legendary football coach of the Green Bay Packers, is highly regarded not just because of the number of times he took his team to victory, but because of his unrelenting focus on fundamentals.

Lombardi is said to have begun every season by reviewing the most basic aspects of the game: "This is a football. These are the grid marks on the field. This is the end zone. This is the field goal post. I am the coach. You are the players." On and on he would go, forcing some of the greatest football players in the world to undergo an elementary schooling in a game they knew inside and out.[5]

But Lombardi, a six-time National Football League champion, knew what he was doing. He needed to remind his players that if they were not masters of the very

---

5 - Phillips, Donald T. *Run to Win: Vince Lombardi on Coaching and Leadership* (New York: Macmillan, 2007).

basic elements of their sport, they would never reach the greater heights to which they aspired.

Like Lombardi's players, we as entrepreneurs must constantly revisit the fundamentals to stay on course. When we keep the fundamentals fresh in our minds, we become more resilient when the situation demands. Conversely, when we let many of our earliest, most fundamental lessons fall by the wayside amid a cacophony of more urgent struggles and demands, we're more likely to lose focus and let obstacles overtake our resilience.

Beyond continuous refreshers in the fundamentals, the best way to build resilience is to keep practicing. Travis and I have found that a particularly effective strategy for building resilience is the "see it, own it, solve it, do it" approach outlined by Roger Connors, Tom Smith, and Craig Hickman in the book, *The Oz Principle*.[6]

The authors recount the struggles of the characters in the classic film *The Wizard of Oz* to take ownership of their problems; instead of taking responsibility, the Cowardly Lion, the Tin Man, and the Scarecrow blame their problems on forces outside their control.

Rather than allowing ourselves to become slaves to the whims of chance, *The Oz Principle* recommends that we overcome challenges by breaking down the process into four simple steps:

1. See It
2. Own It

---

6 · Connors, Roger, Tom Smith and Craig Hickman. *The Oz Principle* (New York: Penguin, 1998).

3. Solve It
4. Do It

For most entrepreneurs, the hardest step is the "own it" step. But it's also the most critical step. Owning our problems places us squarely in the driver's seat and also gives us a powerful incentive for reaching a satisfactory resolution.

When we truly own our obstacles, we are saying to ourselves, "This is something I absolutely must deal with, whether I know how to do it right now or not. I will use online resources, my relationship capital with others, my knowledge gained from past experiences, or whatever it takes to solve this, because I own it. It's my problem."

Travis and I are firm believers in all four steps and consider *The Oz Principle* required reading for anyone interested in developing resilience. For years, I have even hung a sign outside my office that reads, "See it. Own it. Solve it. Do it."

Interestingly, people who develop resilience can expect to reap other side benefits too. In fact, psychologists have shown that resilience can be quantified and correlated to intelligence. In one groundbreaking study, participants were asked to use a simple four-point scale to rate how applicable fourteen general statements were to their own lives, such as, "I get over my anger at someone reasonably quickly." The study found that the more resilient someone is, the more competent and comfortable they tend to be in successfully dealing with people in the real world.[7]

---

7 - Block, J., and Kremen, A.M. "IQ and ego-resiliency: Conceptual and empirical connections and separateness." *Journal of Personality and Social Psychology* 70 (1996): 349-361.

THE 5 CHARACTERISTICS OF A SUCCESSFUL ENTREPRENEUR

Travis ran into a big test of his resilience while serving as CEO of an Internet company. Because his company's Internet services were being transmitted through telephone wires, he was beholden to a major regional telephone company. He was shocked to receive a $232,000 bill one month that he knew couldn't be correct but that the phone company insisted needed to be paid immediately. The phone company threatened to turn off all of his company's services if the bill was not paid in full. This left Travis no choice but to file a lawsuit and obtain a court injunction.

Seven months later, the Public Utilities Commission determined half of the bill was Travis's responsibility, a sum that Travis accepted but that financially constrained the company for a year as he paid off the balance. Throughout the ordeal, however, Travis did not allow his emotions to get the better of him; he looked at the situation logically and strategically, always thinking about the company's best interests over his own emotions.

Limitations of Resilience

As important as resilience is to the success of any organization, every entrepreneur should be aware that there are times when resilience, taken to the extreme, can make problems much worse than they otherwise would be. Sometimes, resilience simply will not solve our problems, and that's why we need to know its limitations.

To help business leaders recognize when resilience is not going to yield the results they have hoped for, we've come up with two key questions every company should answer to help figure out when to throw in the towel. These general questions span all business types and many different situations.

1. Are your efforts to see that your business succeeds having a severely negative impact on your personal or family life?

Anytime your work life is beginning to ruin family relationships, it is time to re-evaluate what you are doing at work and ask yourself if it's really worth it. Obviously, every entrepreneur can expect long hours, tough decisions on a daily basis, and a great deal of stress. This is a normal part of the process of owning a business, particularly if it is a fledgling startup. But if you have already been at it for a while and the long hours are only getting longer, and the financial stress is only becoming more stressful, perhaps this particular business venture may not be right for you and your family.

It is equally important—actually, it is absolutely critical—that, as a business leader, you keep a very close eye on your personal finances. Many young entrepreneurs invest a significant amount of their own resources into making sure their businesses succeed. But you must set personal boundaries to let yourself know when you are getting into a financial situation that could be difficult to pull yourself out of. If you are on the verge of losing your home, for instance, it is probably a good time for re-evaluation.

2. Have you been in business for at least two years, and are you still struggling to maintain a revenue stream?

If you're in a service-based business and you're still burning through cash after being in business for two years, it is probably time to take a good look in the mirror and ask yourself if this is the right business venture for you. (If you're in a product-based business and have venture capital backing, you can probably get away with burning cash even after two years, but you need to keep in mind that you'll eventually need to position your company well to raise the next round of capital.) I have seen far too many instances when a company's biggest problem is not the business model or the product, but rather the founding CEO himself. As a leader, it can be a painful thing to admit that you haven't produced a profit, but when you're able to humbly accept this reality, you can prevent a world of headache and begin transitioning strategically into something different before it's too late.

When Travis and I talk to young entrepreneurs about leaving a struggling company they've founded, they often refuse to seriously consider it. Even after we point out that the business has been around for two, three, four, or five years and yet still cannot sustain revenue growth, the founder will frequently respond by talking about stories he has heard about some other entrepreneur who got by using spare change found in the couch and was eventually successful. What is often forgotten in recounting these stories is that those entrepreneurs were probably at about $5 million in revenue and were bootstrapping their businesses. The allegedly destitute entrepreneurs were, in fact,

Resilience: The Secret Sauce of Success

past the point of proving a product and were not desperate to convince investors of the viability of their product.

Even more troubling, we also frequently see unprofitable businesses that have been around for five years or more where the founder is still taking out investments $300,000 at a time. The founder in these situations tells himself that, following this one-time investment, the company will be profitable in a year, eighteen months, or two years. The problem, of course, is that a business that has been around five years is not likely to suddenly figure out how to be profitable over the next eighteen months.

We're not saying that an unprofitable business shouldn't keep working toward its vision after five years. For instance, a company making $4 million in annual revenue that is breaking even might not be in particularly bad shape. Depending on the industry and business model, a time like this might be a great time to turn on its resilience full force, especially if the business has already solved the riddle of how to bring in revenue consistently. All that remains to be done is to redouble efforts and find a way to turn revenue into profit. This is also a classic example of how a business might prematurely hang up its cleats, quitting when success is just around the corner.

How Resilience Pays Off

For those businesses that demonstrate resilience appropriately, the rewards are plentiful. This is why Travis and I refer to resilience as the secret sauce of success. As we learn and grow from our struggles, as we take on our obstacles with energy, optimism, and clairvoyance, we become primed for repeated, long-term success. The talents, skills, and abilities we obtain prepare us for more advanced obstacles that enable us to reach ever greater heights.

Resilience certainly paid off for me during my first few months at PcCareSupport, the tech company I started from the ground up. As I explained earlier in the book, after months of banging our heads against a wall trying fruitlessly to generate client leads, we decided to think outside the box and try to find a radio station willing to trade services with us—that is, willing to air ads for PcCareSupport in exchange for computer network services.

As I shared at the beginning of this chapter, this new strategy was transformative for us—perhaps too transformative. Very quickly, we started to project all of our hopes and dreams for the future onto this radio station partnership. We all had romantic images in our minds of the radio ads becoming our breakthrough moment, of phones ringing off the hook, of feeling suddenly overwhelmed (in a good way, of course) about handling the sudden influx of new customers.

During the moment the first PcCareSupport ad aired, we dropped everything we were doing. We all began staring at our office phones, waiting for them to start ringing. We felt confident this was going to be the day everything changed for us.

The first few minutes went by without any phone calls, but we didn't bat an eye. Then ten minutes went by and I felt the mood of the office drop a notch.

Fifteen minutes. Still no calls.

Thirty minutes.

Sixty minutes.

The hours kept ticking. Not one single call.

With every minute that went by, I could feel our resilience being stretched to its breaking point. A million thoughts raced through our heads: *What had we done wrong? Did we write a poor ad? Did we choose a bad time to run the ad? Did the station fail to air the ad? Maybe we just haven't fine-tuned our sales pitch. What if we don't have a viable business model? What are we going to do now?*

Then my phone rang, and all eyes turned to me. I answered immediately, midway through the first ring. A sweet, elderly woman told me she had just heard our radio ad and wondered if we could help her solve an issue with her home computer. It would be just a few questions, she promised.

I had no reason not to help her, although I was secretly crushed. PcCareSupport was not in the business of helping individuals with their home computers. We were not even set up to bill someone like her. So I turned her over to one of my technicians, who ended up spending more than an hour answering all of her questions. Every time he would answer her question, she had another. In the end, she thanked him and hung up.

The first day ended with just a few mediocre sales leads. I found myself feeling more dejected and disappointed than I'd ever felt about our business. Still, the idea of doing the radio ad had been transformative for my beleaguered team. We vowed to press on.

A few days later, I received an unexpected phone call. A man on the other end of the line told me he'd heard about the extensive computer support that we'd provided to an elderly female caller at no charge, and that we'd made her very happy. "I'm the chief development officer of the wireless Internet provider Jab Broadband," he continued, "and I wanted to personally tell you thank you. That woman you helped is the mother of my VP of Operations." I was dumbfounded.

That single conversation planted the seeds for a business relationship between our company and his—a highly successful partnership that was the turning point. And the sobering reality is that it may not have happened for us if we hadn't shown unrelenting resilience in the face of our seemingly insurmountable obstacles.

Some pessimists might hear this incredible story and think that we just got lucky, that we happened to be in the right place at the right time. My view of luck is that it's what happens when preparation meets opportunity. Yes, we were fortunate to partner with a large and established company, but it was not by chance. It was our unflappable resilience that gave us the competitive edge we needed.

Furthermore, if we look purely at probabilities, it was one of our competitors that should have been more likely to land the lucrative partnership we got. On paper, this company was more qualified than we were and had been in business for seven years. We were a new startup. Our competitor had a proven track record selling its product. We didn't even have the budget to market ours.

What set us apart is that we worked diligently, patiently, and persistently through obstacle after obstacle, without ever being totally certain how things would work out. Although the going certainly got tough, we did not refuse to help a random caller whom we couldn't even charge for tech support; we did not let budget constraints beat us down; and we owned all of our weaknesses, problems, and struggles. We recognized that nobody could solve our problems but us.

As the leader of this company, I knew it was important for me to be a role model of resilience for my employees during this trying time. Indeed, psychology studies have affirmed that entrepreneurs can have a direct impact on the resilience of their employees. A 2005 study by the University of Nebraska at Omaha demonstrated that people who mentioned their leader as a positive influence when dealing with a difficult or challenging situation exhibited greater resilience than those who did not.[8]

As entrepreneurs, we cannot forget that we don't just play a transformative role in the success of our companies; we also play this role in the lives of our employees.

Travis, as CEO of a major broadband Internet company, once showed up to work to find the tires slashed of every installer truck his company owned. His frustrated employees fretted over how they'd be able to fulfill the more than twenty customer installations they had lined up that day and gossiped that a disgruntled employee had just been fired a few days prior. But Travis didn't allow the cowardly act or speculation about the culprit to overwhelm him. He called up a local tire store and asked for immediate help replacing all of his slashed tires. He coordinated all of his employees to help jack up the trucks and swap out the tires in a rapid, assembly-line fashion. Within an hour, Travis was able to get all of his trucks on the road.

---

8 - Harland, L., W. Harrison, J. Jones, & R. Reiter-Palmon. "Leadership behaviors and subordinate resilience." *Journal of Leadership and Organizational Studies* 11 (2005): 2-14.

Although Travis was well aware of the likely culprit, he did not allow himself to get upset or angry at any point. A month later, he leased a warehouse to provide a more secure location to store all of his company vehicles.

Like Travis, my ability to model resilience to my employees also has been tested. During the early days of Simplus, another tech startup I cofounded, our cash flow was very tight, and we needed to be very careful with our money.

Unfortunately, within a two-week period, we hit a very bad streak of luck that required me to model resilience to my very worried employees. First, Simplus's credit card processor abruptly withheld a large sum of money because we had neglected to alert them to a series of big charges. Then, our controller got duped, in an elaborate fraud scheme, into wiring a big chunk of our cash to a con artist. (In the fraud case, the criminal created a fake email account and used it to pose as me authorizing the funds transfer!)

My employees felt just awful at what had happened and expected me to blame them. Of course I was upset at first, but I quickly calmed down and stressed that we needed to stay focused on the things we could control. By maintaining resilience, I was able to show them there was no need to panic, and, in the end, we were able to recover all of our money.

Putting Resilience into Perspective

At its essence, resilience is the act of working toward one's vision. Resilience acknowledges that, on our journey, we can expect numerous obstacles and setbacks. It allows us to take ownership of these obstacles, to work relentlessly to solve them, and to refuse to stop when it looks inconvenient to continue.

Resilience cares less about satisfaction than it does about reaching success. It foregoes the cheap satisfaction of a short-term win to gain a more complete, satisfying triumph over the long term. Resilience waits patiently while it works, recognizing that tomorrow is always a new opportunity to overcome and learn. And from that perspective, resilience can be the most difficult characteristic to develop of the five we need for entrepreneurial success.

The good news, though, is that resilience can be learned. Although early theories of resilience suggested that this character trait was genetic and some people are just born with resilience, there's now an increasing body of evidence that shows resilience can be learned. Indeed, psychologists have conducted multi-decade studies that demonstrate people can become markedly more resilient over their lifetimes.[9]

In Sum . . .

Resilience is the secret sauce of success. It gives us a path forward as we encounter obstacles, and it gives us an opportunity to continually grow, learn, develop, and thrive. Although we learn resilience at an early age, we often lose this skill by the time we become entrepreneurs. The loss of our resilience is attributed to our failure to respond to obstacles properly, our instant-gratification mindset, and our tendency to dodge accountability. At the same time, we must remember that resilience can only take us so far and that we need to find the proper balance to be optimally positioned for entrepreneurial success.

---

9 - Coutu, D.L. "How resilience works." *Harvard Business Review* 80.3 (2002): 46-55.

ACTION PLAN

1. **Embrace obstacles, challenges, and opposition:** When you encounter bumps in the road, don't become demoralized and allow them to beat you down. Make a conscious effort to view them as opportunities to grow and learn, so you'll be stronger the next time around.

2. **Avoid the wrong ways to view opposition:** Practice spotting the entrepreneurs who don't view opposition the right way. They fall into three main categories: those who impose limits on themselves in response to opposition, those who view opposition as a sign they're losing control of their destiny, and those who seek to obliterate opposition as quickly as possible without learning anything.

3. **Reject instant gratification:** Recognize that the easiest way out is not the way to build work ethic. When you find yourself feeling gratified too often, it's probably coming too easily and at too great a cost.

4. **Avoid deflecting blame:** When you find yourself pointing the finger of blame, stop yourself. You're eroding your own resilience. Remember, as an entrepreneur, the buck stops with you.

5. **Live the "See it. Own it. Solve it. Do it." philosophy:** Obstacles that test our resilience are only obstacles until we break them down into actionable steps. That's the essence of this four-step "See it. Own it. Solve it. Do it." philosophy.

6. **Recognize that resilience can't solve everything:** When your work starts having a negative impact on your personal or family life, or when you're struggling to see any positive signs of revenue growth, it should be a red flag to you. Your resilience might be getting in the way of your personal or financial health—and you need to let go of this unhealthy resilience that's keeping you going when it shouldn't be.

POSITIVE ATTITUDE: BRINGING OUT OUR BEST SELVES

"The sun shines and warms and lights us and we have no curiosity to know why this is so; but we ask the reason of all evil, of pain, and hunger, and mosquitoes, and silly people."

– Ralph Waldo Emerson

If you were to pick almost any random person on the street and ask him or her whether having a positive attitude is crucial to success, you would undoubtedly get the same answer every time: of course, yes.

No one would argue with you that having a positive attitude is a good thing. If you were to follow up, however, by asking these same folks whether they have a positive attitude toward work—and whether their coworkers share this attitude—the answer might no longer be such an enthusiastic "yes."

No doubt we all have worked with colleagues we feel don't share our work ethic, and that's what is most likely to stick out in our minds. When it comes to ourselves, however, we're very likely to believe we maintain a positive outlook toward work.

Since it clearly cannot be that everyone but us is burdened by a negative attitude toward work, there's a disconnect happening somewhere, and we need to understand the source.

Here's what Travis and I believe is really happening: We tend to not see negativity in ourselves and/or are simply in denial about it, even as we readily pick up on negativity in others. Because we struggle to look objectively and systematically at how we act and think, we often don't realize when our attitude is not truly aligned to obtain the outcomes we want out of life.

Our attitude toward work is made up of three ingredients: our emotions, our belief systems, and our exhibited behaviors.[1] We certainly are in control of our belief systems about work, but our conscious belief system is not necessarily in sync with our less-conscious emotions toward work and how these emotions shape our unconscious exhibited behaviors toward work.

This gets to the heart of the disconnect. We are often helplessly out of sync—and yet blissfully unaware we are out of sync.

Thus, the first step to correcting a disconnect is to pause and come to a greater understanding of what it truly means to have and maintain a positive attitude.

---

1 · Di Martino, Pietro, and Rosetta Zan. "What Does 'Positive' Attitude Really Mean?" *International Group for the Psychology of Mathematics Education* 4 (2003): 451-458.

In this chapter, Travis and I will seek to turn your understanding of a positive attitude upside down as we analyze this seemingly simple—but actually incredibly complex—concept. Next, we will explore both the upsides and downsides of negative emotions in shaping our attitude. We will also discuss the importance of adaptability in the workplace as it relates to maintaining a positive attitude over the long term. We will close out this chapter by listing the many benefits of a positive attitude and the important role that a positive attitude plays in our success.

What Our Survey Reveals about Positive Attitude

At any moment, something terrible, unexpected, and potentially life-altering could come crashing into our lives that could change the way we view our work and the world. During these upsetting, confidence-shattering, and extremely frustrating times, we come to depend on a positive attitude to maintain our focus toward achieving our goals and vision.

The business CEOs and founders who responded to our survey understood the importance of attitude when they selected positive attitude as the fourth most important characteristic of entrepreneurial success. About one out of every three survey respondents (34%) selected positive attitude as one of the five key traits.

In their comments to us, our survey respondents emphasized that the road ahead for entrepreneurs is hard and that bumps in the road will invariably test one's spirit and resolve.

"Don't forget to enjoy the ride," one respondent wrote. "It's a series of ups and downs, so make the best of the ups and try not to get too down in the down times."

"Hang on in good times and bad," another respondent wrote.

Positive attitude was most likely to be selected by business CEOs and founders who have been in business two to five years, with 53% in this category selecting this characteristic. The next most likely group to select positive attitude was those who have been in business six to ten years.

What our survey respondents were conveying to us is that, as entrepreneurs, our attitude can mean the difference between being able to hang in there when the times get bad and not being able to stay afloat.

Building Blocks of Attitude

A positive attitude starts with having confidence in yourself. A self-confident individual is ready and eager to build up those around him in a way that benefits everybody. People with self-confidence know that whatever struggles may come their way, they will be able to cope with those struggles and find a way to overcome and learn from them.

Still, confidence is not synonymous with positive attitude; a confident entrepreneur is not necessarily a positive entrepreneur.

In the workplace, psychologists who have studied employee attitudes have sought to understand how to measure positive attitude. Psychologists have come up with a number of behavioral characteristics they believe can help explain why some people have a more positive attitude than others.

In a 1980 psychology paper, researchers from the University of Sheffield in the United Kingdom advanced the theory that individuals' attitudes toward their workplace can be measured by weighing three factors.[2]

1. Interpersonal trust at work

The more trust that is engendered between individuals and teams within an organization, the more positive the employee's attitude will be toward his or her employer.

2. Organizational commitment

The stronger the feelings of attachment that an employee has toward the goals and values of his organization, the more positive the employee's attitude will be toward his or her employer.

3. Personal need non-fulfillment

The more an employee longs for a personal need that is not fulfilled by the organization, the more negative the employee's attitude will be toward his or her employer.

In a 2014 paper, psychologists at Eastern Michigan University advanced a slightly different, more simply stated trio of components that can be used to measure job satisfaction. The authors argued that all three are significantly positively correlated with job satisfaction.[3]

---

2 - Cook, John, and Toby Wall. "New work attitude measures of trust, organizational commitment and personal need non-fulfillment." *Journal of Occupational Psychology* 53.1 (1980): 39-52.

3 - Young, Lauri, et al. "The tenuous relationship between salary and satisfaction." *Journal of Behavioral Studies in Business Volume* (2014).

To maintain a positive attitude over the long term, therefore, entrepreneurs cannot afford to operate on autopilot. We need to be engaged, to draw meaning and positive feelings from our work at all times. That said, it's not realistic to be positive about everything all the time, and that's where we need to understand the value of negativity.

1. **Meaningfulness:** The employee needs to feel that work is meaningful.
2. **Responsibility:** The employee needs to feel that he has responsibility for work outcomes.
3. **Knowledge:** The employee needs to feel that he has salient knowledge of his work.

What's clear from these theories about positive attitude is that for entrepreneurs to build a foundation for a long-term positive attitude, entrepreneurs cannot afford to operate on autopilot.

They need to be engaged so they can draw meaning and positive feelings from their work at all times. This is perhaps the essence of every employees' formula for success at work, and it's particularly crucial for entrepreneurs, who really cannot afford to have a bad week or even a bad day!

However, it's not realistic or healthy for entrepreneurs to be positive about everything all the time. Rather than try to avoid negativity altogether (an impossible task), the best thing to do is to confront it head on and turn it into an asset.

The Importance of Negativity

Let's face it. Our emotions are a difficult thing to control. If we feel negatively, we cannot pretend to feel positively. If we try to engage in too much happy talk, it's just going to feel forced and so far removed from reality.

How, then, do we prevent ourselves from working so hard to maintain the appearance of a positive attitude that we begin to suppress and ignore our true feelings?

Perhaps the best way to think about our attitude is to view attitude as being the sum of discrete elements. Some elements will be positive, and some will be negative. Therefore, each element either adds to or subtracts from our abilities to reach our goals and achieve our vision.

In other words, not every feeling we have is positive, and that's OK. The goal is that these elements should collectively be in the positive—and, ideally, as positive as possible.

Here's an example: Let's say you find out you didn't achieve a major milestone you were hoping to achieve. Of course you'll be disappointed; it's unrealistic to, like Pollyanna, skip along your merry way and pretend nothing happened. This feeling is a negative element, and you must subtract it from your overall attitude.

But from your disappointment and sense of defeat, you can draw strength and be propelled forward. When you adopt a positive, determined mindset, you've just canceled out your negative element and come back into the positive.

Psychologists have affirmed that negative feelings can be a source of strength and growth. Although it may seem counterintuitive, researchers have posited that negative emotions resulting from our own blood, sweat and tears are actually at the core of our growth.

Furthermore, researchers say, the negative emotions we experience in the middle of a frustrating, trying time tend to feel less negative after the fact. What happens is that, in hindsight, our minds instinctively tend to look at our challenges as opportunities to achieve growth and happiness. Thus, we remember the feelings associated with those times as being much more positive than they originally felt.[4]

Psychologists also have come to view a negative attitude as a tool that can help us self-regulate the pursuit of our goals. The theory is that when our negative emotions overwhelm our rate of return, it serves as a signal to us that we should re-evaluate the pursuit of our goal.[5] The takeaway message here is that although we might be able to make it through a challenge that engenders nothing but negative feelings in us, it may not be the best thing to blindly plow through. We must learn to listen to that little voice inside our heads—the one that clues us in when a challenge might not be worth surmounting.

While negative attitudes within us can be important drivers of success, we certainly don't want to surround ourselves with external negativity. Unfortunately, too many of us seems to have too much of it.

---

4 - Talevski, Marina. "So Bad That It's Good: The Role of Negative Emotions in Happiness." *Editorial Team*: 65.

5 - Randolph M. Nesse. Natural Selection and the Elusiveness of Happiness. *Philosophical Transcations-Royal Society of London Series B Biological Sciences*, pages 1333-1348, 2004.

Avoiding Negativity Around Us

Travis and I have attended countless lunches with entrepreneurs and other business leaders who talk incessantly about the things going wrong in their businesses. They gripe about what they don't like about their company, their coworkers, and their responsibilities.

Every time we see this happen, we are disappointed. We wonder what happens when these leaders return to work after lunch, remarking to each other that it's hard to believe that someone who has just bemoaned everything wrong with their professional life can possibly be in the right mindset to be kind, patient, and encouraging to those they lead. Even if they've just received some disappointing news before the luncheon, griping about it won't help them respond to the news in a productive way at work.

Of course, it's possible that many of them just needed to get something off their chest. But our respect toward these folks who unload on us is diminished, and we are not more likely to do business with them; in fact, quite the opposite is true. Perhaps most disappointing, though, is that we almost never leave these lunches feeling happy, upbeat, or encouraged.

The reason all of this is so troubling is that so much of our attitude is dependent on our ability to avoid becoming trapped by the depressing, demoralizing perspectives and behaviors that surround us.

At the same time, for whatever reason, we, as humans, are instinctively drawn to negativity and the things that bring us down and are prone to ignoring the many things we do that uplift us. Ralph Waldo Emerson famously expressed this sentiment when he wrote, "The sun shines and warms and lights us and we have no curiosity to know why this is so; but we ask the reason of all evil, of pain, and hunger, and mosquitoes, and silly people."

Thus, we must recognize that we're in a constant battle against ourselves to avoid negativity and stay focused on positivity.

When we recognize this weakness in ourselves, we also can begin to wade into others' negativity and turn the liability in front of us into an asset. The most powerful example for me of turning a frown into a smile came a few years ago. I was playing a game of pickup basketball with some business acquaintances, and an unresolved dispute between two players suddenly boiled to the surface. They had been caught up in something before our game that had nothing to do with the game, yet they were bringing their frustration and negativity to the court and bringing down everyone.

As the pair began verbally taking swipes at each other, I realized our game would be in jeopardy if they couldn't simmer down. So I took a deep breath and, as calmly as possible, walked up to them and said, "Hey, guys. It's going to be OK. Let's not worry about it here. Everybody here is healthy and OK. We're just having some fun, playing a game." For whatever reason, the simplicity of my message resonated with them, and the tension we had all felt on the court suddenly vanished.

I probably would have forgotten all about this situation had one of the players involved in the scuffle not turned out to be the CEO of a company with which my company was very interested in partnering.

I initially didn't think we had a chance at this partnership because his company did not have a track record of entering into these types of partnerships. But during our first meeting together shortly after that basketball game, I could tell he was as interested in this partnership as I was. He was incredibly receptive to meeting with me and to hearing my ideas, and our companies ended up building a strategic partnership that became extremely lucrative for both of us.

During our negotiations, I asked him point-blank why he was interested in going down a path with me that his company wasn't known for taking. That's when he shared with me that he had not forgotten about the basketball game where I intervened and put a stop to his petty fight with another player.

"I saw the way you handled that tense situation," he said, "and I thought, 'I want to do business with that guy.'"

Although I didn't think I had done anything particularly remarkable, I realized it was my positivity that had made him look at our fledgling company from a different perspective. Our company might not have ended up entering into that partnership without it.

I recognize that we all need to complain, to vent, and to air our frustrations if we hope to get past them. I need to do it too. My point is simply that we need to be cognizant of how and where we're doing our venting, and to recognize that we need to minimize complaining for the sake of complaining.

To me, complaining is one of the easiest things in the world to do. Complaining is, at its core, an admission of weakness and incompetence. It reminds us of things that are frustrating and unpleasant that we have no control over—things that we need someone (or something) else to do to resolve for us.

How many centuries have we as a society wasted lamenting the vicissitudes of mortal life before we finally decided to go figure out a way to live longer and happier? Anyone can point out every last injustice in the world, but it's the individual who is willing to work to change those injustices who makes a lasting difference.

Positive Attitude Requires Adaptability

When I started my vending art supplies business, I personally serviced my highest-volume vending machine. I would wheel my inventory into a back room for storage, then restock the machine at night. Some of the employees who worked in this building I knew from high school, and they would talk down to me, thinking I was just a stock boy.

That didn't bother me, but what did alarm me was when someone started taking my merchandise from the locked storage room. Although I asked for the lock to be rekeyed, the building manager refused. I wanted to keep my vending machine there, and I certainly did not want to accuse anyone of stealing, so all I could do was maintain a positive attitude.

Eventually, after the thefts kept happening, I moved all of my inventory out of the back room and brought only what I needed each night to restock my machine. Through it all, I was friendly to everyone who worked at the building and continued to share the joys of running this business with anyone who took an interest in what I was doing.

One day, someone who worked in the building approached me about making an offer on my business. I ultimately sold it to him—for three times the revenue it was bringing in! For me, this was a powerful lesson in how a positive attitude can give us the clairvoyance to navigate obstacles—and ultimately to chart our way to success.

Throughout the business world, when life declares a foul ball, it is so important for us to be able to evaluate as many options as we can. The leader who insists on an unchanging set of goals because they were on his original list is a leader who will not accomplish very much.

Unfortunately, it's all too common for entrepreneurs to focus on something they really want and then fail to realize there could be multiple routes to get them to their end goal.

Let's use basketball as an analogy. You might come up with the best play in the world to outsmart your opponent, but when your opponent messes up your play, you don't have time to mourn your losses and declare you can't achieve your goal of winning. You need to be adaptable, evaluate the changed circumstances, reconsider your options, and make whatever adjustments are necessary.

Indeed, every good basketball player understands she has an entire playbook of options to choose from every time her teammates bring the ball up the court, as well as a huge repertoire of skills and tricks that can be used to help her team score a basket.

When goals are set in stone and we refuse to reconsider them, we cannot anticipate or plan to make adjustments and refinements to them; thus, we put our positive attitude at risk. Successful leaders recognize that goals require adjustment and refinement along the way. Often they require many adjustments and refinements.

Having said this, Travis and I want to add some important perspective. First, we're not saying that every original goal is a bad goal that will eventually need to be refined. Many times, our first goals are the right goals. Second, we're not arguing that you shouldn't feel some strong emotions—especially passion—toward achieving your goals. These feelings can provide you with the extra fire and determination you need to overcome the obstacles that will come your way.

The problem is that when you become too emotionally attached to your goals, you run the risk of not being able to adjust fast enough to curb the inevitable dip in your attitude. And that's a problem, because a positive attitude requires lots of ongoing maintenance.

Benefits of Positive Attitude

Most entrepreneurs believe they have a positive attitude. Even people who consider themselves "realists" or "pessimists" tend to view their attitudes as positive. As long as their attitude is enhancing their ability to achieve their goals, they're convinced their attitude is positive.

But when you spend time around a truly positive, uplifting person, it is a transformative experience. You find yourself truly inspired to change the way you go about doing everything and, indeed, the way you think about and view your life.

The truth is that having a positive attitude is one of the most coveted, respected traits in the business world. Unfortunately, it's also one of the most elusive. Most people don't understand that they're losing the battle against their own negative selves, and they also don't seem to appreciate why it's worth making a proactive investment in positivity.

Travis and I routinely extoll the power of positivity in the workplace, and for good reason. There are tremendous advantages. Let's take a closer look at them. A positive attitude can help you . . .

1. Transform the attitudes of those around you.

As entrepreneurs, we need to be a positive influence on our employees to achieve our goals, and a positive attitude is one of the best ways of doing that. Simply put, a positive attitude is infectious. People who associate themselves with positive people are more likely to become positive people themselves. When we respond to the most difficult situations in a positive way, it inspires others around us to be equally optimistic, positive, and helpful. In contrast, the more time we spend with someone who has a negative attitude, the less time we are going to want to be around that person, and the more we are going to be uninterested in that person's work and leadership habits. While we can get away with spending a little bit of time with such people, too much time can leave us feeling poisoned.

2. Meet more people who are positive.

The more time you spend with a positive person, the more you are going to want to introduce that person to some of your friends so that they can enjoy his or her company too. While you may have some personality differences, and your tastes and preferences will differ from the other person's, these are easy to overlook and manage precisely because positive people know how to avoid dwelling on these trivial differences.

3. Build the entrepreneurial spirit of others.

As entrepreneurs, our success is shaped by the success of those who work for us. Our employees need to share our value systems and our entrepreneurial spirit to accomplish wonders and create something out of nothing. Studies have confirmed that a positive entrepreneurial spirit rubs off on others. In a 2008 psychology study of 4,413 college-aged students, students who were immersed in an educational environment that encouraged entrepreneurship were more likely to possess stronger entrepreneurial inclinations. Specifically, the study showed that the attitudes of these budding entrepreneurs toward their professions were greatly influenced and shaped by their teachers, parents, mentors, and role models.[6]

4. Get your projects back on track.

A positive leader brings a hefty dose of uplifting energy that can fill an entire team with excitement and determination about completing a great challenge. That's because

6 - Todd, Davey, and Aurora Teixeira. "Attitudes of Higher Education students to new venture creation: a preliminary approach to the Portuguese case." FEP Working Papers (2008).

positive people focus on the possible. They maintain a razor-like focus on what can be, rather than on what is or what can't be, won't be, or shouldn't be. We've all heard the saying, "Misery loves company," but Travis and I believe the real saying should be, "Misery only loves company for so long." When employees are ready to brush themselves off and get back on track, they need the company of a positive leader to propel them forward.

5. Avoid the vicious cycle of excuse-making.

People with negative attitudes focus on things outside their control, which triggers an endless cycle of blaming, complaining, and excuse-making. They react with great alarm to even the smallest of problems. No bump in the road is too small for them to share how bad it is with everyone they know. When we consider how easy and natural it feels to get sucked into this vicious cycle, it's no wonder that the more time we spend around people with a negative attitude, the more likely we are to develop a negative attitude ourselves.

6. Extend your influence.

Have you noticed that people with a positive attitude seem to exert a far greater influence on others than those with a negative attitude? Their circle of friends and associates is larger, their successes are more frequent, and their accomplishments are more meaningful. This is particularly ironic because negative people exert tremendous effort into sharing (and persuading others to adopt) their way of thinking. Positive people, on the other hand, don't waste their time; they go about their duties and let the results speak for themselves.

7. Gain clairvoyance to overcome adversity.

A positive attitude has the power to help us see more of the options available for dealing with our problems. When we are motivated by fear, anger, frustration, jealousy, impatience, and other negative emotions, we become blind to solutions that do not satisfy the demands of our negative emotions. Behavioral writer James Clear uses a particularly good analogy to explain this phenomenon. He says that if we were to encounter a tiger on a forest trail, our brain would respond to the fear we feel by focusing entirely on the tiger and how we can get away from it. This fear, Clear argues, causes us to narrow our mind and focus our thoughts. Although this response is useful from an evolutionary perspective, shutting out the rest of the world every time we encounter a problem is counterproductive and hurtful to us. "Your brain closes off from the outside world and focuses on the negative emotions of fear, anger, and stress—just like it did with the tiger," Clear writes. "Negative emotions prevent your brain from seeing the other options and choices that surround you."[7]

While no one would argue that a positive attitude is beneficial, the hard work of fostering this attitude within ourselves takes work on our part. We must fight proactively against our own innate tendencies to be attracted to and to wallow in our own negativity.

---

7 - Clear, James. "The Science of Positive Thinking: How Positive Thoughts Build Your Skills, Boost Your Health, and Improve Your Work." *Huffington Post*, July 10, 2013. http://www.huffingtonpost.com/ james-clear/positive-thinking_b_3512202.html, accessed 8/8/2014.

Living a Positive Attitude

When I'm faced with a frustrating situation that has the ability to put a damper on my attitude, I try to stay focused on the big picture and figure out whether this is really something worth allowing my attitude to take a hit over. I ask myself three questions:

1. *Is this life or death?*
2. *Is this a large problem in the grand scheme of things?*
3. *Do I need to get involved for this to work out?*

When I asked myself those three questions and realized the answer to all of them was no, I calmed down and moved on. These three simple questions have the universal ability to make the stresses and frustrations in your life a whole lot less stressful and frustrating. Even if you ultimately decide that you need to intervene (at the cost of your attitude, no less), this mental exercise can help you gain a better perspective on the situation and make a more objective decision.

Travis and I focus on maintaining a positive attitude in our daily lives by focusing on three things: perspective, gratitude, and a positive support system. The three questions above ensure that we are able to step back, remove our emotions and deal with the task at hand. It's amazing how small and manageable any issue becomes when you remove the emotion from it.

To maintain my sense of gratitude for everything I have—as cheesy as it sounds—I own a Gratitude Rock. It's a rock that is a physical reminder of all the good things in my life that surround me, including all of the amazing opportunities that I have to give back to family, friends, and employees.

Finally, I maintain a positive support system by rejecting negative people (to put it bluntly) and surrounding myself with positive people. I simply don't believe in making room for negativity in my life and workplace. I know they don't contribute anything to me, and their toxic attitude doesn't allow for growth.

In Sum . . .

The attitude we maintain as entrepreneurs can have a transformative effect on us and those around us. A positive attitude can bring immense strength and pride, or we can allow our positivity to be dampened in the negative forces that we're instinctively attracted to and that inevitably bring us down. When we learn how to turn negativity into a positive or reject it outright, when we recognize the many benefits of maintaining a positive attitude, we are setting ourselves up to bask in the glow of a powerful trait that radiates from within us and helps us to accomplish great things.

ACTION PLAN

1. **Stop being in denial about your own negativity:** Acknowledge that it's not just other people who express negativity toward work, but you, too. The sooner we can identify the negativity in ourselves, the better we can work on channeling it effectively.

2. **Aspire to draw meaning and significance from your work every day:** To build a positive attitude toward work, you want to build up trust among colleagues, find projects and tasks that you can commit to fully and have mastery over, and identify responsibilities that instill pride in you.

3. **Recognize that negativity can shape and bolster a positive attitude:** Stop suppressing and being ashamed of your negative feelings; they can actually be a source of strength and growth. Sometimes they will even prevent you from going down a path you shouldn't be taking.

4. **Avoid the negativity of others:** You should be working proactively to avoid others' negativity for two reasons: so it doesn't infect your life, and so you can intervene when there's a chance you can put a stop to someone else's negativity.

5. **Be adaptable and flexible:** If you find yourself thinking things can only be done one way, force yourself to come up with another way. The more

adaptable and flexible you are, the less likely you are to be disappointed, and the more likely you are to maintain a positive attitude.

6. **Draw inspiration and motivation from positivity's benefits:** When you're down, think about how much happier and more successful you'll be if you can turn your frown into a smile. You'll be more inspiring, more productive, more influential, and more ready to overcome adversity.

PASSION: THE FUEL FOR ENTREPRENEURIAL INTENSITY

"The first step is to establish that something is possible; then, probability will occur."

— *Elon Musk*

Tammy Bowers is the personification of entrepreneurial passion. Several years ago, the Utah Valley mom rolled out a personal medical record-keeping service that allows caregivers to input and organize medical information in a smartphone app that syncs to the cloud.

Tammy's company, LionHeart Innovations, was inspired by her young son, Landen, who needed a heart transplant at three months of age. When a distraught Tammy and her husband asked their son's surgeon what they could do to optimize his chance of survival, the surgeon offered them this sage advice: be involved in your son's medical care.

Tammy took this advice to heart, and it has fueled her passion to not only be proactive and diligent about tracking her son's complex and dynamic medical history, but also to share her best practices, technology-driven approach with other parents and caregivers in similar situations. From this simple idea, LionHeart has quickly evolved into a successful tech startup offering a sleek, user-friendly smartphone app at no cost to users.

Travis and I were fortunate to be among the early investors, and I assure you it was an easy investment decision for one simple reason: I could feel the incredible passion she has for her business.

Psychologists have described entrepreneurial passion as the intense commitment we feel for our business endeavors that stems from our ability to visualize a successful enterprise. But, as any entrepreneur will tell you, generating this level of commitment and sustaining it over the long term can be elusive for many of us. The reality is that entrepreneurial passion requires just the right combination of support from loved ones, the right circumstances and education, and the right environment.[1]

Being truly passionate about something can mean the difference between success and failure. Passion keeps us motivated and driven, sets ourselves up for success, and ensures we're able to bounce back when tough times hit. Without passion, we set ourselves up for negativity to creep in and stall our dreams.

---

1 - Liao, Jianwen, and Harold Welsch. "Entrepreneurial intensity." WB Gartner, KG Shaver, NM Carter, & PD Reynolds (Eds.), *Handbook of Entrepreneurial Dynamics* (2004): 186-196.

In this chapter, we start by examining why passion is so remarkable and transformative, including what my survey of business CEOs and founders reveals about passion. Next, we take a look at the important ways that passion transforms our lives and our workplace, and how to effectively cultivate it. Finally, we launch into an important discussion about the limitations of passion and the ways that it can be detrimental to our entrepreneurial endeavors.

What Our Survey Reveals About Passion

Passion is the fuel of entrepreneurial intensity, and indeed, the CEOs and business founders who responded to our survey were keenly aware of this. One in three of our 2,631 respondents selected passion as one of the five most important characteristics of entrepreneurial success.

"The truth is, anyone can become an entrepreneur when they are willing to learn at a rate of adaption," one survey respondent told us. "What I mean by that is you need to learn everything about your dream in order to bring it to life. Believe in what you are doing, and take it to the end."

No matter how long an entrepreneur has been in business, passion is consistently identified as a top trait necessary to achieve success. The age bracket most likely to select passion was the entrepreneurs who have been in business two to five years. One in two of these survey respondents picked passion.

Meanwhile, at the other end of the spectrum, the age bracket least likely to pick passion was the entrepreneurs who have been in business for a year or less; even so, nearly one in four of them picked passion, reaffirming that even in the earliest stages of a startup–where we can barely tell our right hand apart from our left hand–passion is viewed as an important component of entrepreneurial success.

"Find a passion, find a dream, and go get it," one survey respondent told us.

Another pointed out that for the best outcome, we should always trust our passion to steer us in the right direction.

"Act on your best impulses; ignore the retaliatory ones," this entrepreneur told us. "You'll sleep better and end up with better long-term results."

Passion Fuels Your Energy Level

When I entered middle school, I desperately wanted to make the basketball team. Because my basketball skills were lagging, I knew I wouldn't make the team unless I practiced four to five hours each day–more than any of my friends were doing. Although 300 students tried out, I ended up as the solo alternate pick, and I couldn't have been more thrilled; to me, simply making the team was enough–and proof of the power of passion.

The passion we feel as children for even inconsequential things works the same way in the workplace. When you are passionate, you work harder than anybody else. Sure, you'll always have competitors and critics who are smarter than you, have more capital than you and develop a better strategy than you, but when you exude passion, you feel empowered and confident, like you're ready to go head-to-head with any of these folks. And indeed, that's often the essential fuel you need to find success.

In the book *The 5 Laws That Determine All of Life's Outcomes*, motivational speaker and noted entrepreneur Brett Harward recounted that one of his most eye-opening experiences was when he received a knock at his door from a self-assured young man. Although Harward instinctively assumed this man was trying to sell him something, the young man instead stated he was simply seeking some advice. He hoped to own a home in Harward's neighborhood one day, so he wanted Harward to tell him about the kind of people who lived in the neighborhood and the choices they'd made in their lives that enabled them to afford to buy homes there.

Harward didn't advise the young man that he needed to go to an elite college or to switch his profession to something extremely lucrative. Instead, Harward offered this wisdom: "Create maximum value wherever you're at right now. Bring that attitude to your work, your relationships, your hobbies, and you can cut your climb up the hill by 90%."[2]

What Harward was trying to communicate to this young man was that being afforded special privilege and opportunities in life was not what gave people in his neighborhood their competitive edge, but rather that they had passion—all day, every day.

To me, this young man already was exuding his passion. If he was willing to go out of his way to knock on doors

---

2 - Harward, Brett. *The 5 Laws that Determine All of Life's Outcomes* (Salt Lake City: FranklinCovey Publishing, 2008).

and gather the information he was looking for, then he no doubt would be able to channel his energy to break through the ranks in his workplace, find success, and ultimately earn enough income to afford a home in his dream neighborhood.

Researchers have demonstrated the important role that passion plays in fueling interest in entrepreneurial endeavors specifically. In a 2012 study of 946 Canadian university students, passion was shown to strengthen how people perceive their ability to become successful entrepreneurs, as well as the attractiveness of this role. The study found that the passion with which they undertook work-related activities invigorated and enhanced their entrepreneurial intentions. The authors concluded that the more passionate an entrepreneur is about work-related activities, the more likely they are to exploit their current knowledge base and reap the accompanying feelings of joy and self-accomplishment.[3]

When you're passionate about something, the reality is that it's constantly on your mind, helping you to recognize connections, patterns, and events that move you closer to your goals.

Noted venture capitalist Bobby Genovese is a prime example of an entrepreneur whose passion drives everything about his work and life. His zeal for life comes from connecting enthusiastic people to winning opportunities. He has parlayed this unabashed passion for work into two venture capital firms with global reaches, plus a number

---

3 - De Clercq, Dirk, Benson Honig, and Bruce Martin. "The roles of learning orientation and passion for work in the formation of entrepreneurial intention." *International Small Business Journal* (2012): 0266242611432360.

of side projects, including real estate and a museum for antique boats.

"His passion is life itself in every aspect, as he tackles and blocks the road less traveled," the biography on Genovese's website reads.

When you exude passion, it's amazing how your vision and goals start to come up in conversations, how networks start to be made, and how you begin to form connections, both external relationships and internal connections in your head, that help you to process and solve problems. You simply cannot afford to miss these opportunities; your success depends on it.

Passion Provides Clairvoyance to Solve Problems

I was once part of a startup company that began with $5,000 and a handful of cofounders—all of us with families to feed. I'm not convinced, however, that we would have been better off if we'd had access to more cash or to bigger credit lines.

That's because our desperation and fear allowed us to accomplish some pretty amazing things. With a paucity of resources at our disposal, we were forced to get extremely creative. We needed to learn how to market our product, to generate sales leads, to pay our bills, to grow as a company—all without that one "crutch" that could have transformed our predicament in an instant (i.e., money).

Passion often works in this manner; it keeps entrepreneurs in a problem-solving mindset as they tackle some of the most overwhelming, unexpected challenges of their lives. Passion also helps us find and attract others who come to us with fresh new ideas and valuable perspectives.

And perhaps best of all, everything you learn about how to apply passion can be applied again and again in your life. For me, experiencing the way that passion transformed my successes in the early part of my career has given me the clairvoyance to solve challenges at my current company. And my current successes in solving problems, in turn, have continued to fuel my passion.

Passion Draws Out the Best in Others

When Travis and I create a vision and blueprints for a startup company, the last thing we want to do is hide it from the world. But that's exactly what far too many entrepreneurs do. They feel that their ideas will be poached or that they'll expose themselves unnecessarily to the competition.

It's all nonsense, of course, and here's why: The more you're open to sharing your vision and your passion with others, the more they'll be attracted to you and start thinking about how they can support you (while presumably supporting themselves, of course). Not everyone you meet is going to be supportive and positive, but over time you'll learn how to target your message to the type of audiences who can help you.

Sharing your concept with a positive, supportive audience also will give you a mental payoff. As you put yourself and your ideas on the line and let your passion shine through, you will enjoy validation through the approval of others. Furthermore, the people you've shared your passion with become the people who hold you accountable in a positive way. Once you share your ideas with others, they come to count on you to deliver on your ideas.

Finally, your passion will attract new talent to you. Prospective employees who might be dissuaded by the newness of your ideas or turned off by your lack of experience will be inexplicably drawn to you. This is the effect of passion on others.

The passion effect has helped Travis and me with recruiting top talent countless times over the years. People simply enjoy being around people who are confident and focused on their passion. In our case, a passion for our businesses rubbed off on prospective hires, convincing them to take an interest in what we were trying to accomplish.

By contrast, when you fail to convey a confident, genuine passion for your work, those around you will instinctively pick up on it. They will feel it, and they will pass along those feelings to everyone you hire. People don't want to get behind someone like that, and the end results will reflect it.

As much as your passion can fuel the enthusiasm of those around you, it's not a miracle drug. In fact, there's such an imperfect correlation between entrepreneurial passion and its effects on others that researchers have been working in earnest to parse out the nature of the relationship.

In a 2012 study of employees who work for German startups, for example, researchers questioned the prevailing wisdom of entrepreneurial passion from the top having a consistently positive trickle-down effect on employees. The study, which was conducted by the Technische Universität München in Munich, divided the passion that entrepreneurs exude into three distinct categories: passion that is derived from founding the business, passion derived from inventing new products and services, and passion derived from improving and developing organizational and business processes. The researchers then correlated the level of each type of passion with the response it engendered in the entrepreneurs' employees.

The study found that the three categories of passion do not all have the same impact on employees' attitudes and commitment to work. While passion for inventing and passion for improving business processes had a positive impact, passion for founding did not have a comparable positive impact. Hence, the authors concluded that when an entrepreneur is merely passionate about founding his company, this passion will not have a rubbing-off effect on his employees and, consequently, will be statistically unlikely to improve employees' attitude and commitment levels.[4]

Different types of passion aren't the only reason that passion can have less than desirable effects. Researchers have also found that passion may not have a positive influence on one of the most important things that startup companies need: venture capital funding. According to the findings of a 2009 study by the University of Washing-

4 - Breugst, Nicola, et al. "Perceptions of entrepreneurial passion and employees' commitment to entrepreneurial ventures." *Entrepreneurship Theory and Practice* 36.1 (2012): 171-192.

ton and Wichita State University, funding decisions made by venture capitalists regarding promising startups have nothing to do with how passionate the entrepreneur is; rather, they have everything to do with the preparedness of the entrepreneur.

This study, which looked at aspiring entrepreneurs in college and a group of professors who judged the students' funding pitches, found that passion was not positively correlated with venture capital funding decisions, whereas preparedness was correlated positively. The authors concluded that while passion is important to sustaining the venture over the long term, passion could be less valued by venture capitalists because funders aren't necessarily convinced that passion itself can translate to sales.

Even beyond this startling finding, the venture capital study also offered interesting insights into how we perceive and quantify passion in entrepreneurs. The study used what is known as the Perceived Passion Scale to quantify an entrepreneur's passion level. The researchers measured the following key elements that make up an entrepreneur's passion: energetic body movements, rich body language, animated facial expression, liberal use of gesturing, a face that lights up when speaking, and varied tone and pitch.[5]

It's interesting that these mannerisms, which at first glance seem rather superficial, can actually serve as meaningful indicators of entrepreneurial passion.

---

5 - Chen, Xiao-Ping, Xin Yao, and Suresh Kotha. "Entrepreneur passion and preparedness in business plan presentations: a persuasion analysis of venture capitalists' funding decisions." *Academy of Management Journal* 52.1 (2009): 199-214.

How to Cultivate a Passion for Entrepreneurship

Elon Musk's passion for space travel started with a conversation with a fellow entrepreneur during a roadtrip. Musk had made a fortune on PayPal and was searching for a new place to put his investment dollars.

After his initial conversations about partnering with the Russian space industry did not go as hoped, Musk decided he was going to move forward alone by starting his own company. His roadtrip companion, accomplished entrepreneur Adeo Ressi, recalled trying to talk Musk out of his idea—the crazy idea that became SpaceX.

"We wound up literally having an Alcoholics Anonymous-style intervention, where I flew in people to Los Angeles," Ressi told Esquire magazine. "And we all sat around a room and said, 'Elon, you cannot start a [rocket] launch company. This is stupid.'"

"Elon just said, 'I'm going to do it. Thanks.'"[6]

By 2006, Musk had a $278 million agreement with NASA to start putting humans in space.

As Musk's story so vividly illustrates, passion for entrepreneurship starts with passion for an idea that could provide a tremendous benefit to society. Musk's passion for the idea of space travel—and what it might mean for the survival of the human race on other worlds—is what propelled him to create SpaceX against tremendous odds.

Motivational speaker Jack Canfield once said, "When you are happy doing what you love, you've already won.

---

6 - Junod, Tom. "Elon Musk: Triumph of His Will." *Esquire*, December 2012. http://www.esquire.com/news-politics/a16681/elon-musk-interview-1212/.

When you do something you love with passion and perseverance, you are already a success."

To define your passion, begin by asking yourself what takes up most of your time. What activities make you feel most happy? What tasks feel most rewarding? In your spare time, what news and industries do you follow?

Next, you want to evaluate the broader market and industry to decide if you truly have—or could develop—a passion for this line of work. The truth is that if you don't have a passion for what you are doing, you will not succeed. You will lose focus, you won't sustain your work ethic, and you will struggle when difficulties and tough decisions arise.

Travis and I have seen far too many entrepreneurs who choose their so-called passion in accordance with whatever business idea has dollar signs written all over it. But their passion invariably fizzles within the first year, or as soon as they encounter their first big obstacle. The end result is that they give up.

Hence, before you move forward with your startup idea, ask yourself: Is this something I want to build something around? Am I willing to do what it takes to realize this passion?

Often, you'll find yourself in Elon Musk's shoes, with multiple trusted confidants telling you not to move forward with your outlandish idea for a space travel company. Maybe they're right; maybe you're right.

When you're in this predicament, just dip your toe into your area of interest. Don't quit your day job. Just explore your passion and treat it initially as a hobby. Let it develop over time and see what happens. All along the way, you'll get cues as to whether you're on the right track. If it's the right thing for you and its potential starts to pan out, you'll want to keep going, and your passion will guide the way.

For Travis and me, our passion is ignited by all of the projects that our day jobs have allowed us to pursue on the side. For instance, I'm interested in developing software to foster positive culture within companies and to help make work more fun. Although my initial investment in this project isn't likely to immediately translate into financial rewards, I'm motivated by the possibility that, one day, it will turn into something that could make a difference in peoples' lives. And with this success will come profitability.

Travis and I also work as angel investors for the investment firm, JW Capital. We love this work because we're motivated by our desire to see fellow entrepreneurs succeed so that we can collectively strengthen our businesses and our communities as a whole.

The Dangers of Passion

Not all passion is healthy. Passion motivated by anger, spite, or revenge will destroy your business. Passion that leads you to abandon common sense, your ethics and values, or your dignity will never sustain you over the long term.

Psychologists have long recognized that unbridled passion can be unproductive and potentially detrimental. In a 2011 joint study between the U.S. and Singapore, psychologists advanced the theory that workplace passion falls into two distinct categories: harmonious passion (the healthy kind) and obsessive passion (the unhealthy kind).

Harmonious passion, the researchers explained, develops in response to a love for one's job that stems from within, rather than from external pressures or recognitions. In contrast, obsessive passion—the type of passion associated with workaholics—is a passion that drives us to work so hard that we become controlled by it and that triggers other aspects of our life to be negatively impacted by it.

To illustrate the difference, the authors described two software engineers who appear to be equally passionate about their work. The one with harmonious passion is driven to find success by keeping up with advancements in various programming languages and by researching and writing his own programs. The one with obsessive passion, on the other hand, is driven to find success by positioning himself as the go-to guy at his workplace for help with high-level software issues; he thrives on being perceived by others as an invaluable asset.

What's the difference? The first engineer is able to pursue his job voluntarily and can distance himself from his job when necessary; the second engineer experiences guilt and anxiety when he's not doing or thinking about his job, because his perceptions of success depend on constant reinforcement from others.[7]

Therefore, we ideally should aim to exude only harmonious passion for our endeavors; practically, though, we're inevitably going to be a little obsessive at times. The takeaway message here is that we should be cognizant of the

---

7 - Ho, Violet T., Sze-Sze Wong, and Chay Hoon Lee. "A tale of passion: Linking job passion and cognitive engagement to employee work performance." *Journal of Management Studies* 48.1 (2011): 26-47.

difference and aim to keep the scales tipped toward harmonious passion as much as possible.

The evidence about the limitations of passion don't end here. Psychologists also have posited that too much of any form of passion can be detrimental. In a 2009 academic paper published in the *Academy of Management Review* journal, psychologists made the case that passion that is too positive or intense can actually be a hindrance to the creative problem-solving abilities of an entrepreneur.

The root of the problem, the authors explained, is that the entrepreneur comes to love the intensely positive experience so much that he becomes resistant to exploring alternate options, a crucial trait when looking for creative new solutions to challenges. The authors concluded that the optimal amount of passion to have is somewhere in the middle. Have too little, and it will kill his chances of success. Have too much, and it will overwhelm his creative problem-solving abilities.[8]

Everything in moderation, right?

When to Stop Your Passion in Its Tracks

It's one thing to recognize the different types of passion and their limitations. It's an entirely different thing to know how to relate these principles to real-world situations. Although there is no magic formula to understand passion's role in our lives, we can start by keeping two things in mind.

---

8 - Cardon, Melissa S., et al. "The nature and experience of entrepreneurial passion." *Academy of Management Review* 34.3 (2009): 511-532.

First, we must recognize when our passion is leading us to sacrifice and compromise our values, our core beliefs, our health, our relationships, and our families. We must seek to find balance in all things in our lives, and this is especially true when it comes to passion.

For example, a 2014 study by a Stanford University researcher found that productivity among munition factory workers fell sharply after a fifty-hour workweek, and dropped even more dramatically after fifty-five hours.[9]

Second, we must recognize fluctuations and shifts in our passion level. If our passion is waning, if we find ourselves becoming easily distracted or unfocused about what it is that fuels our passion, then we must be prepared to react to it appropriately. For example, we may find our passion waning because our skill set is no longer a good match for the business or because we're struggling to take the business to the next level. Whatever the reason, we must be prepared to accept that it may be time to do the unthinkable: to sell our company and move on to our new endeavor.

Sometimes the best thing we can do is to walk away from our businesses, to find somebody else who has more passion to take the reins. Even the most dedicated of entrepreneurs develops an exit plan. The key is to make your exit a part of your overall business plan, a way to culminate a job well done.

When a friend of mine entered the tech startup market, his exit plan evolved as the market evolved. He followed the industry trends and was aware when the computer

---

9 · Pencavel, John. "The Productivity of Working Hours." IZA Discussion Paper No. 8129 (2014).

industry as a whole started heading toward mobile. Because he knew his passion and energy would not be a good match for the evolution to mobile, he used the mobile revolution as the basis of his exit plan. And indeed, when the time came for his business to undergo the mobile revolution, he bowed out and sold his company.

As entrepreneurs, we're often reminded that timing is everything in business. Well, the key here is that our timing is dictated by our passion. Passion drives where you stand, where you're headed, and where you'll end up.

Sustaining Your Passion

When we're first starting a business, we need a lot of everything—a lot of energy, a lot of enthusiasm, a lot of commitment and, of course, a lot of passion. In a 2005 article in the *Journal of Business Venturing*, researchers posited that passion in the early stages of a business is not only what makes work fun, but also what offsets the sparse and nonexistent monetary rewards in those earliest days. Without passion, an entrepreneur can become so detached from the immense challenge of starting a business that failure becomes inevitable.[10]

But once you've persevered through the early stages and found some measure of success, how do you sustain the same passion over the long term? It was easy and natural to obsess over your labor of love in its infancy, to spend every waking moment thinking about it. But once the most challenging of obstacles to creating a successful

---

10 · Cardon, Melissa S., et al. "A tale of passion: New insights into entrepreneurship from a parenthood metaphor." *Journal of Business Venturing* 20.1 (2005): 23-45.

startup has been overcome, an entrepreneur can be left with a rather anticlimactic existence, and at this point, it's not uncommon for your passion to dim.

The solution is to constantly be looking for new opportunities that rekindle that original passion. For some, it's as simple as creating new divisions or branches of the business; for others, it's about finding what Travis and I call auxiliary endeavors that build upon prior successes but feel uniquely entrepreneurial. Often, an auxiliary endeavor takes the form of a charitable foundation, which also can double as a financial shelter for the main business! Charitable foundations are almost like starting a new business, requiring an entirely new vision that comes with a new set of goals and challenges.

Noted venture capitalist Bobby Genovese, who founded BG Capital Group and headed up the Canadian Beverage Company, is perhaps best known for eventually turning his attention to establishing charities. Chukkers for Charities, a nonprofit corporation, supports various children's organizations in the southern Florida area, while SickKids has become one of Canada's leading pediatric cancer research centers. Through these endeavors, Genovese has been able to savor the thrill of the entrepreneurial chase again, while also doing tremendous good for his community.

In Sum . . .

Passion is essential to success, transforming our attitudes, our businesses, and the way others perceive us—including our own employees. While following our passion is always the right instinct, it cannot be done blindly, as not all passion is healthy or productive. Still, passion is behind all successful entrepreneurial ventures. As legendary Apple cofounder Steve Jobs put it once, "The ones who think they are crazy enough to change the world are the ones that do."

The key to changing the world is to define and understand the importance of passion. It will fuel your ability to recognize and act upon opportunity, and it will allow you to surround yourself with helpful, supportive people. When you realize your passion, the whole world stands to benefit from your vision of a better tomorrow.

ACTION PLAN

1. **Recognize that passion is the essential fuel for entrepreneurial success:** Think about the most successful people in life. What do they all have in common? They exude passion. Learn to live like the most passionate people in the world.

2. **Use passion to overcome obstacles:** Passion gives us clairvoyance to solve problems, if we let it. Whenever you can't solve a problem, put your problem aside and focus on reinvigorating your passion for your business. Once your passion is reinvigorated, that problem will no longer feel so insurmountable.

3. **Realize that passion is palpable:** The next time you listen to an inspiring speaker, focus on the way the audience reacts and the things you feel inside. It's a great firsthand lesson in the inherent transferability of passion.

4. **Work proactively to flesh out what gets you passionate:** Ask yourself what activities take up most of your time, make you feel happiest, and feel most rewarding. Then, analyze the broader market or industry and figure out whether what you feel passionate about can be parlayed into a business venture.

5. **Understand how to avoid the unhealthy kinds of passion:** To reject the types of passion that are detrimental, pay particular attention to obsessive behaviors in yourself and view them as red flags. The last thing you want is to be controlled by your passion or to have your life become negatively impacted by it.

LIVING THE FIVE CHARACTERISTICS

"Our greatest weakness lies in giving up. The most certain way to succeed is always to try just one more time."

— Thomas Edison

Serial entrepreneurs like Elon Musk embody the spirit of the American success story. With the development of PayPal, Musk ushered in a revolutionary new way to buy things online. With SpaceX, he paved the way for a new golden age of space exploration, aiming to make it cheaper and easier to put humans into space. And as head of Tesla, Musk upended the auto industry by carving out a luxury niche market for electric vehicles.

These high-profile ventures have made Musk an extraordinarily wealthy man, and, indeed, he could have retired on the fortune he's made from any single one of his ventures. But as Musk has made clear many times, money isn't what motivates him to work. Musk's goal is to fundamentally shake up and improve the lives of ordinary people with each of his ventures, and he's willing to give his all to ensure this happens.

"If you have millions of dollars, it changes your lifestyle," Musk declares, "and anyone who says differently is [lying]. I don't need to work, from a standard-of-living point of view. But I do, you know; I work every day and on weekends, and I haven't taken a vacation for years."

What Musk embodies is not the relentless pursuit of profit that permeates our business climate, but rather entrepreneurial success in its purest form—a synergistic, harmonious blend of vision, work ethic, resilience, positive attitude, and passion. Musk understands that to live a truly entrepreneurial life, our motivation to work must not be money. Instead, our motivation must be our desire to create a positive domino effect for change. Where others see insurmountable obstacles and challenges, true entrepreneurs see opportunity to make transformative progress and advancement. Money and success will follow.

In this chapter, we open with a discussion about how we can learn to live the essential characteristics of entrepreneurial success. Next, we explain how to apply these characteristics to common situations and challenges that we as entrepreneurs often find ourselves in. And we close with some inspiring words of wisdom that we hope will keep your feet firmly planted on the path to success, no matter what curveballs life may throw your way.

Learning to Live the Five Characteristics

There is no direct path or clear formula for becoming a successful entrepreneur, but that doesn't mean we must flounder aimlessly as each of us reinvents the wheel from scratch. Those who have come before us have much wisdom to offer, and they are at the heart of our own ability to find success.

In our survey of business CEOs and founders who have earned at least $1 million in annual revenue, more than 2,600 of them told us loud and clear that some character traits are much more important to possess than others. Thus, it's incumbent upon us to learn to live these traits in our daily lives, especially the five characteristics most commonly selected by our survey respondents. Here, again, are the five characteristics:

Living with Vision

Entrepreneurs who live with vision are constantly thinking about their long-term goals. They push past fears, uncertainty, and self-doubt to stay focused on achieving their dreams. Vision is their roadmap, a path that keeps them moving forward even when the going gets rough.

Living with Work Ethic

Entrepreneurs who live with a strong work ethic relish in the satisfaction of good, old-fashioned work. Day in and day out, they toil diligently and relentlessly, aware that wishful thinking and easy shortcuts do not produce long-term results. They learn to view work as its own reward.

Living with Resilience

Entrepreneurs who live with resilience embrace obstacles and challenges as opportunities to learn and grow and ultimately succeed. They understand that resilience is a mental game that is won over a long period of time. The secret to winning is to never make excuses and blame others, but rather to keep one's eye on the prize at all times.

Living with a Positive Attitude

Entrepreneurs who live with a positive attitude thrive off being engaged in their work and drawing meaning and emotional sustenance from it. They understand how dramatically and wholly a positive attitude can transform their pathway to success. They reject the negativity that surrounds them and do not let emotionally charged situations bring them down.

Living with Passion

Entrepreneurs who live with passion feel an intense commitment to their endeavors that stems from visualizing success. Indeed, passion is the fuel of entrepreneurial intensity, ensuring that entrepreneurs sustain progress toward their goals. With passion, entrepreneurs stay motivated and driven and are able to bounce back when tough times hit.

Living these five character traits covers the essential bases we need to succeed as entrepreneurs. We need vision to understand and be reminded what all of our efforts are for. We need work ethic to provide meaningful results that empower us to keep moving forward with our vision. We need resilience to enable our work ethic and to remind us of the vision we are working toward, especially when the going gets tough. We need a positive attitude so we don't stray from the strong work ethic that is essential to achieving our vision. And we need passion to inspire and fuel our work ethic and resilience on our road to achieving success.

As you can see, all of these traits are interlinked. It's essential that we recognize the relationships between these traits and are continually self-aware of how we can influence our own destiny by maintaining a razor-sharp focus on these traits. When synergistically applied in our lives, these traits give us the most important qualities we need to combat all that life throws at us.

Applying the Five Characteristics

Throughout our professional lives, Travis and I have encountered many situations where the five characteristics helped us solve problems and move forward. We've also seen how the five characteristics are interwoven into the success stories of our peers and how a lack of these characteristics defines stories of failure and shortcoming.

As soon as we're able to recognize the five most important elements of entrepreneurial success, we can learn how to apply them appropriately and accurately to real-life situations. Let's explore some of the many ways that the five characteristics can guide us through situations that we, as entrepreneurs, commonly find ourselves in.

Thinking outside the box

In the early days of a startup, when you face incredibly limited budgets and no name recognition, it can be tough to sell your product or service. How do you get past the frustration of this experience? The solution is to think outside the box, to get past the self-pity, and to exercise some resilience and work ethic. When you and your team are devoted and focused, you're able to put on your creative thinking cap and figure out the solutions you need.

Overcoming depressing days

Everyone has down days. Travis and I certainly have them. The road to entrepreneurial success is long and hard, and it often requires us to assume great risk that does not always pay off–at least not right away. Fortunately, because we focus on exuding a positive attitude, we inspire a positive attitude in our employees. They, in turn, help us to get through our down days. In this way, we help one another to maintain our passion for what we're trying to accomplish.

Knowing how fast to grow

When you start a new company, your goal isn't (or shouldn't be) to immediately sell your product or service to every household in America. You need to hit a certain stride for how fast you'll grow, and for that you need to know where you want to go. With vision, you're able to flesh out a multi-step plan to incrementally take you to where you want to be. Your passion and work ethic will see that plan through.

Recognizing the importance of timing

Several years ago, Travis had an opportunity to sell a business he'd headed for sixteen years. Travis understood the business better than any buyer. He could climb a transmission tower to fix an outage himself just as easily as he could tell you the reputation of every vendor in the industry. But he also understood the law of diminishing returns, and he knew his business wasn't going to grow, so he exited at one of the highest multiples in the industry. Just as his passion fueled his company's growth, his vision ensured that he would not become so emotionally attached to the company that he would pass up the opportune moment to part ways and sell it. And indeed, he was proven right, as that business wasn't able to grow by much more. Timing is everything in business, and vision ensures you can recognize it.

Prioritizing goals

As we work toward finding success in business, we typically set a series of goals and objectives, and we seek to measure our outcomes against these objectives. Unfortunately, in the chaos of running a business day after day, it's easy to set too many goals or goals that conflict. That's where our mastery of vision becomes crucial. With vision, we're able to distinguish and prioritize the goals that matter most. We gain the clairvoyance to rank our goals and establish which ones are our shorter-term, more intermediate goals and which are our longer-term, most significant goals. When we understand which goals matter most, we're able to more effectively judge our performance and our progress toward those goals.

Helping you stay focused

Once you have established your company and added all of the people and elements that are necessary for it to succeed, your job as a leader is to stay above the management fray and keep your eye on the prize. If you have truly done everything you can to make sure you've hired the right people, it should be easy to maintain this focus. Unfortunately, entrepreneurs often become distracted by many of the day-to-day challenges that are an essential part of having a successful business. Therefore, you need your vision to stay on track and your work ethic to give you structure.

Admitting you have a problem

Far too many entrepreneurs fall into a trap of either ignoring their problems or denying their existence. Like dealing with grief, the first step is denial—and if we can never move past this first step, we can run our businesses into the ground. If we do not see the obstacles before us, how can we ever expect to overcome and learn from them? This is where a well-articulated vision comes into play. A true vision includes recognizing obstacles and having a plan to resolve them. Once we can acknowledge a problem, we rely on other traits, especially resilience and a positive attitude, to steer us through the problem and successfully emerge at the other end.

Inspiring change in yourself

Everyone has bad habits that affect performance and the success of a business. When we recognize the things we want to change about ourselves, we impose accountability on ourselves. Once we have this accountability, we can apply our work ethic and resilience to successfully implement the changes we seek in our lives.

These are just a sampling of the many ways that living the five characteristics helps you to find success in your entrepreneurial endeavors. In every action you're pondering, in every decision you make, the five characteristics should be supporting you and pushing you toward achieving your goals.

Living for Success

When Travis and I began writing this book, our motivation was not to make money. (As any author will tell you, writing books is a tough way to earn a living.) Instead, we saw a need to shed new insights on how to make it in today's entrepreneurial business world and how to create a project that could shine a light on an issue that vexes us all in the business community.

Although some of our peers questioned our return on investment for such a superfluous project, we believed in what we were doing—we still believe in what we're doing—because we know it has the potential to make an important mark on the entrepreneurial business world. Thus, at every step of the way, it was not even a question that we would devote ourselves fully to this project and see it to fruition.

When we live the five characteristics—vision, work ethic, resilience, positive attitude, and passion—all of our endeavors can, and do, have the same outcome. We are living for success, refusing to let anything bring us down, and taking life's challenges in stride. Rather than dreading obstacles and opposition on our path to success, we can persevere through these experiences, knowing that we're learning vital lessons along the way. Rather than getting distracted by the things that don't matter, we can focus on the things that do matter, knowing that the latter will keep us on the road to success. And rather than second-guessing every decision we make, we can trust ourselves to get it right the first time, or the second time, or however many times it takes.

Through it all, when you live to achieve success, you will find your way.

In Sum . . .

Learning to live the essential characteristics of entre-preneurial success starts with understanding vision, work ethic, resilience, positive attitude and passion. Once we have this understanding, we can begin applying these characteristics to common situations and challenges we face as entrepreneurs. As we learn to apply the character-istics effectively, our entrepreneurial success becomes an inevitability. It's just a matter of when.

ACTION PLAN

1. **Set in motion a domino effect for positive change:** True entrepreneurs don't work for money; they work because they believe in positive change. Work on letting go of your obsession with making money; the financial rewards will flow just as soon as you create truly positive change.

2. **Practice living the five characteristics:** The business CEOs and founders who responded to our survey gave us a list of the five characteristics most essential for entrepreneurial success: vision, work ethic, resilience, positive attitude, and passion. Use their wisdom to develop these personality traits thoroughly and carefully.

3. **Practice applying the five characteristics:** Think through the multitude of ways that the five characteristics can be applied to real-life business situations. From overcoming depressing obstacles and setbacks to recognizing the importance of timing, the five characteristics can be widely applied to help navigate all sorts of difficult, complex, and sensitive situations.

CONCLUSION

Despite the evolution and maturation of the business world in recent decades, businesses continue to depend on entrepreneurial leaders. Yes, managers and executives make most of the day-to-day decisions that keep a company on track and growing, but entrepreneurs are the only ones who can truly take us from point A to point B and who can make the world a better place simply by being an entrepreneur.

In the book *The 7 Habits of Highly Effective People*, Stephen Covey uses a simple but powerful analogy to illustrate the difference between an entrepreneurial leader and all of the other employees of a business.

"Envision a group of producers cutting their way through the jungle with machetes," Covey writes. "They're the producers, the problem solvers. They're cutting through the undergrowth, clearing it out. The managers are behind them, sharpening their machetes, writing policy and procedure manuals, holding muscle development programs, bringing in improved technologies and setting up working schedules and compensation programs for machete wielders."

And what about the entrepreneurial leader? "The leader is the one who climbs the tallest tree, surveys the entire situation and yells, 'Wrong jungle!'" Covey writes.

"But how do the busy, efficient producers and managers often respond? 'Shut up! We're making progress.'"

In our modern age, with so many demands constantly clamoring for our attention, time, and effort, we remain in desperate need of prescient leaders capable of climbing to great heights, surveying our landscape, and steering all of the managers, producers, and other employees in the right direction.

To become this leader, we must learn to be the best entrepreneur we can be, to recognize and build our capacity for the most essential characteristics of entrepreneurial success. That's why the roadmap to entrepreneurial success that our survey respondents have provided all of us is such a game-changer.

They told us we need vision to know how to move forward and get past obstacles in our paths.

They told us we need a strong work ethic to toil daily and diligently toward our goals, without unrealistic hope of an easy shortcut.

They told us we need resilience to power through obstacles and challenges and ultimately to find success.

They told us we need a positive attitude to remain engaged in our work and to be emotionally fulfilled by it.

And they told us we need passion to provide the essential fuel we need to achieve our goals.

A Career Like No Other

Not long ago, I was sitting in a meeting with my talented leadership team. At one point, our discussion turned to my role as founding CEO of the company. As they shared with me their admiration for how far we'd come, I remember throwing out the following question only half-jokingly: "Would you want to succeed me as CEO?"

They all reacted swiftly and in unison, "No, absolutely not."

I don't believe they said no because I work significantly longer hours than they do; indeed, many of them are working every bit as long and hard as I am. Rather, their reaction was so visceral and emphatic because they are intimately familiar with the decision-making pressures on me every day–the big, company-altering decisions that can make or break all of us.

While we, as entrepreneurs, thrive on this pressure, most of our colleagues want to avoid it at all costs. In the dog-eat-dog world of business, one or two bad decisions by the CEO can topple an entire company and cost all of its hardworking employees their livelihoods through no fault of their own.

The executives who work under entrepreneurial leaders understand this reality well. Indeed, Travis and I have seen more than our fair share of startups crumble and fold, and the end result is always the same. Everyone realizes the CEO is to blame. This CEO invariably withers away with shame and embarrassment, like a goalie at a soccer game who fails to block a play that everyone but him saw coming.

Still, the intense pressure on us to not fail is a good thing. It motivates us to work hard every day, to stay on top of our game. Being an entrepreneur certainly isn't for everyone, but for those of us who realize it is our calling, entrepreneurship embodies for us everything that is wonderful and exciting about work. Entrepreneurship is the ultimate opportunity to, in the immortal words of *Star Trek*'s intrepid trailblazers, "boldly go where no one has gone before."

In popular culture, the entrepreneur is typically depicted as a clean-shaven executive in a suit and tie who meets with deep-pocketed investors in a fancy board room. But Travis and I believe this narrow definition of entrepreneurship represents only a tiny fraction of all the entrepreneurs in the world.

Take ancient Greek mathematicians like Pythagorus, Archimedes, Ptolemy, and Euclid. Most people probably would not think of them as entrepreneurs, but we would argue they are. They worked incredibly hard to find solutions to problems that were limiting our progression as a society and, in doing so, they laid the foundation for our exponential advances in mathematics, engineering, and science. Their entrepreneurial spirit is, at its essence, the ideal that all of us as entrepreneurs aspire to—a way to change the world in our own industry, in our own creative way.

The mathematician Euclid, in particular, also seems to have understood what we entrepreneurs are reminded of every day: there is no way to get around consistent, hard work. In an often-told story that reminds us there are no shortcuts in life, Ptolemy I, a Macedonian ruler of Egypt, asked Euclid if he could learn geometry without going through Euclid's lengthy text. Euclid famously replied: "There is no royal road to geometry."

On our own long, winding, frustrating, demoralizing, obstacle-laden road to entrepreneurial success, we must keep in mind that the road we're on is the only road that will get us to where we want to go.

We must prepare ourselves for this journey by building a tightly crafted vision, an unflagging work ethic, a boundless resilience, an internally radiating positive attitude, and a bottomless supply of passion.

With these characteristics, we will not fail because we cannot fail. Success is our final reward on this exciting, endlessly rewarding adventure.

ABOUT THE AUTHORS

Ryan Westwood is an accomplished entrepreneur, educator, mentor, and community leader and philanthropist. An Inc. 500 CEO, Mr. Westwood successfully exited two start-up companies before age 30 and does angel investment work through JW Capital. He presently serves as CEO of the SaaS company Simplus. Mr. Westwood is an inspirational speaker and prolific author whose work has been featured in Forbes, Inc., The Wall Street Journal, and other national business publications. His website, Ryan-Westwood.com, serves as a community resource for fellow entrepreneurs, offering news, analysis, and advice about critical issues in entrepreneurship.

Travis Johnson owns and manages a commercial real estate portfolio in excess of $24 million and serves on the board of directors for several companies, including Simplus, PcCareSupport, Eco Flower, and LionHeart

Innovations. Long drawn to the technology sector, Mr. Johnson got his first Apple computer at age 12, obtained his Certified Novell Engineer certificate at age 19, and founded one of the largest wireless Internet Service Provider companies at age 24. He was recognized with the Outstanding WISP Operator award in 2007. Mr. Johnson also serves as co-founder and managing director of JW Capital, an angel investment group that accelerates the growth of start-up companies.

INDEX

C

Cantner, Uwe 15
Cardon, Melissa S. 144, 146
Carnegie, Andrew 54
Carroll, Lewis 23
Chen, Xiao-Ping 139
Chukkers for Charities 147
Ciavarella, Mark A. 15
Clear, James 124
Collins, Jim 66, 67
Connors, Roger 92
Cook, John 111
Coutu, D.L. 103
Covey, Stephen 163, 164
culture 31, 32, 34, 38, 40, 41, 60, 61, 62, 63, 142, 166

D

da Vinci, Leonardo 3
De Clercq, Dirk 134
Di Martino, Pietro 108
Driessen, Martyn P. 16

E

Eastern Michigan University 111
Edison, Thomas 4, 5, 54, 77, 151
Emerson, Ralph Waldo 107, 115
Euclid 166, 167

F

Falcone, Thomas 64
Forbes Magazine 28, 40

G

Genovese, Bobby 134, 135, 147
goals 17, 26, 31, 49, 71, 75, 88, 89, 109, 111, 113, 114, 119, 120, 121, 134, 135, 147, 153, 154, 157, 159, 164, 165
Good to Great 66, 67
Google AdWords 33
Guadalupe, Manzano 79

H

Harland, L. 101
Harrison, W. 101
Harward, Brett 133
Hébert, Robert F. 14
Hickman, Craig 92
Hill, Roger B. 51

The 5 Laws That Determine All of Life's Outcomes 133
The 7 Habits of Highly Effective People 163
The Ant and the Grasshopper 53
The Oz Principle 92, 93
The Wall Street Journal 28
The Wizard of Oz 92, 93
Thompson, John L. 15
Todd, Davey 122

U

University of Georgia 50
University of Nebraska 101
University of Sheffield 111
University of Washington 138

V

V2MOM (Vision, Values, Methods, Obstacles, Measures) 28, 29, 30, 31, 32, 33, 34, 35, 36,
        37, 38, 39, 40, 41, 42, 43, 44, 45
values 29, 31, 32, 37, 42, 43, 44, 111, 142, 145
venture capital 25, 96, 134, 138, 139
venture capitalist 134, 147
vision 17, 19, 20, 21, 22, 23, 24, 25, 26, 27, 28, 29, 30, 31, 33, 34, 35, 36, 37, 38, 39, 40, 42, 43,
        44, 59, 60, 61, 62, 63, 65, 66, 67, 68, 69, 71, 77, 86, 90, 97, 102, 109, 113, 135, 136,
        147, 148, 152, 153, 154, 155, 156, 157, 158, 159, 160, 161, 164, 167
vision statement 29, 30, 40
Vogelgesang, G.R. 81

W

Wall, Toby 111
Walton, Sam 26
Warner, Marina 85
Welsch, Harold 130
Wichita State University 139
Wilfling, Sebastian 15
Wired 28
Woehr, David J. 52
Wong, Sze-Sze 143
work ethic 17, 21, 47, 48, 49, 50, 51, 52, 53, 54, 55, 56, 60, 63, 64, 65, 66, 68, 69, 70, 71, 72,
        73, 74, 75, 104, 108, 141, 152, 153, 154, 155, 156, 158, 159, 160, 161, 164, 167

Y

Yao, Xin 139
Young, Lauri 111

Z

Zan, Rosetta 108
Zwart, Peter S. 16